Pinch

- Project - "anglersharks"
  Dark chocolate.

Amaco carved porcelain.
blue ski... (high fired and)
unglazed

Knobbly planter
- raw clay
oxide wash
semi matt finish

* Perhaps one of these
enlarged could be a
cinnamon/cocoa shaker.

Bowls

#1 Stoneware with oxids.

c/w white slip honey glaze

marbled?

mot of resist leaves

Replacement

#1a

pressed
indent
suggestions?
Celadon
porcelain

spotty "s/ware

#2 swoopy

#3 Honey + white slip?

cut rim

Amaco

#4 ridges - tingway

coarse stoneware
or white tinglaze
o/ c/w

applied
ridges

glaze wash
(cobalt)

natural g clay

"groovy bowl."

cut rim
(+2).

#3a

light blue-os

amaco ses raised.

Bumps

Amaco

ar fu

4 -65
  -10
  -15

03

e/owed compartment.

...ive Trays

...ve. T

Pinch
POTTERY

Functional, Modern Handbuilding

Susan Halls

LARK

An Imprint of Sterling Publishing
1166 Avenue of the Americas
New York, NY 10036

ISBN 978-1-4547-0413-3

Library of Congress Cataloging-in-Publication Data

Halls, Susan.
  Pinch pottery : functional, modern handbuilding / Susan Halls.
    pages cm
  Includes index.
  ISBN 978-1-4547-0413-3
  1. Pottery craft. I. Title.
  TT920.H3244 2013
  738.1'4--dc23
                              2012042571

Distributed in Canada by Sterling Publishing
c/o Canadian Manda Group, 664 Annette Street
Toronto, Ontario, Canada M6S 2C8
Distributed in the United Kingdom by GMC Distribution Services
Castle Place, 166 High Street, Lewes, East Sussex, England BN7 1XU
Distributed in Australia by Capricorn Link (Australia) Pty. Ltd.
P.O. Box 704, Windsor, NSW 2756, Australia

For information about custom editions, special sales, and premium and corporate purchases,
please contact Sterling Special Sales at 800-805-5489 or specialsales@sterlingpublishing.com.

Email academic@larkbooks.com for information about desk and examination copies.
The complete policy can be found at larkcrafts.com.

Manufactured in China

6 8 10 9 7 5

larkcrafts.com

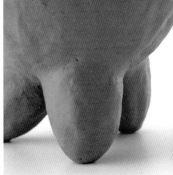

INTRODUCTION

The instinct to pinch: it's a natural response where clay is concerned. Give a child a piece of the soft stuff, and he or she will automatically start to nip and mold it into a little plate or bowl. Many of us became acquainted with clay in this fashion—as kids at school or summer camp, where we produced thumb pots, misshapen pinched-clay vessels that we proudly showed our parents.

My own first encounter with clay involved just such a clumsy pot. Later, I had the good fortune of being taught by an instructor who guided me in the ways of working with pinch pots and opened my eyes to their hidden potential. This knowledge has stayed with me throughout my long career as a ceramicist. It's one of the reasons I was inspired to write this book. As you'll soon discover, the technique of pinching, which uses easy shaping and molding actions, can produce innovative, practical pottery—pieces that rival anything made on a potter's wheel.

The pinching technique has a long history. There is evidence that it was the means by which early man made the first pots. As far back as 3000 B.C., the Naqada culture in Egypt produced small, thin-walled vessels that were scooped out and pinched to refinement. Pinching does seem like a logical first step in the evolution of vessel making—hence the introduction in summer camp!

But—history and ancient cultures aside—why pinch? What makes the technique so special? I believe there are several reasons. First of all, the method doesn't require any equipment. Although a few basic potter's tools can help you enhance your pieces and construct them with more finesse, for the most part, you only need your hands.

Another benefit of the technique concerns skill. Pinching is a slow, methodical way of working, a process that allows you plenty of time—time to make decisions and time to make changes and adjustments. When you pinch, you have much more control over the clay than when you coil or throw. Of course, you'll need to practice. But even if you've never pinched before, you'll find that your fourth or fifth attempt at a simple bowl will show dramatic improvement. You'll be able to move forward very quickly and join two shapes, and then your options will really open up.

"As you'll soon discover, the technique of pinching, which uses easy shaping and molding actions, can produce innovative, practical pottery—pieces that rival anything made on a potter's wheel."

One of my goals with this book is to demonstrate the versatility of the pinching method, to show the level of sophistication that you can achieve by using it. Many of the projects featured in the chapters to come look so elegant you'd be hard pressed to know that they were pinched. That polished look is only one of many aesthetic choices at your disposal. Degrees of finish and refinement are personal decisions—you may want your work to be textured and slightly asymmetrical, displaying visible evidence of the pinching process. You may want to use different colors and glazes than the ones I used. Think of the projects as starting points to fire your imagination and feel free to mix and match ideas and introduce new discoveries of your own.

If the idea of surface treatments seems a bit overwhelming, don't worry! I've included a section on surfaces that dispels the myths and fears so often associated with the subject. You'll learn how to make decisions regarding glazes and patterns and realize that exploring this area of creativity can be fun.

A word of advice: If you want your pieces to be functional and durable, you'll need to fire them in a kiln. In the chapter

on kiln usage, you'll see that the device is unintimidating. The small kiln shown there was used to fire many of the pieces on these pages. Some models can simply be plugged into a household outlet like a microwave.

As you make your way through this book, keep in mind that success comes in small steps. Spend time working on basic shapes. Practice each of these several times until you become familiar with the different pinching actions and the ways in which pressure is critical to successful shaping. Before long, you'll start working instinctively. I suggest that you attempt the mug or trio planter first, and then tackle more complex forms.

Pinching seems simple, and it is. Yet the results are anything but elementary. The techniques that you're about to learn can be used to produce sophisticated ceramic art. Making a pot, though, is only half the story. Pinching is an intuitive response to the material at hand, an action that's deeply rooted in our instincts. So don't be afraid to get your hands dirty! Let the impetus to create in clay inspire and guide you as you work.

PINCHING THE BASIC FORMS

Forming pinched shapes is an instinctive and natural process that allows for endless variation of form. Cones, tubes, bowls—these basic shapes you can create easily, and, for additional variety, make them longer, rounder, and wider. Alter them even further by cutting, adding texture, or pinching to shape. Some shape variations can be adapted into lids, feet, and pouring spouts. Used in various combinations and sizes and in conjunction with composite forms, shape variations represent an infinite number of pot possibilities.

Master the following techniques and you'll not only be able to make all the projects in this book, but you'll be fueled with ideas for new pieces.

ESSENTIAL SHAPES

Before you attempt any of the projects, you would be wise to master the making of these simple, yet essential, shapes. They are your core pieces for most of the projects. Begin with the classic pinch pot, make it several times over before moving on to the sphere, wide bowl, etcetera.

The Classic Pinch Pot

1 Start with a lump of soft clay about the size of a large apple, or whatever feels comfortable in your hand. Pat and slap the clay gently with the palm of one hand while slowly rotating the clay in the palm of your other hand. The intention here is to make a well-rounded form. Any wrinkles or folds must be smoothed out or they will enlarge and tear open as the form begins to grow. Work swiftly so as not to dry out the surface of the clay.

2 Support the ball of clay in your cupped palm. Keep the thumb of your other hand straight and push it deep into the clay, but don't go through to the other side! How much thickness you leave at the bottom depends on what you intend to make and how large the piece will be. I suggest leaving approximately ¼ inch (6 mm) of thickness [A].

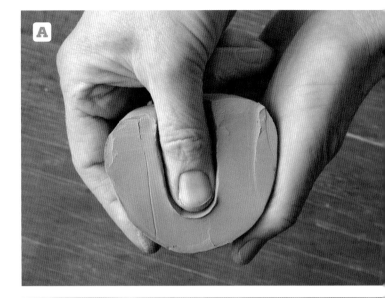

3 Now to make this crude pot into something more elegant. Support the clay in the cupped palm of one hand, then place the thumb of your other hand inside with all the other fingers joined together on the outside. Working from the base, begin to press your thumb and fingers together, rotating the clay after every pinch. Don't rush and don't jump about with your fingers! The turning of the clay should be slow and rhythmic; this will ensure more symmetry to the form. Keep in mind the shape you're aiming to make—I think of this basic pinch pot as resembling half an egg. Once you've pinched the lower area, spiral the pinching action upwards to encompass the sides [B & C]. Keep the pressure between your thumb and fingers equal, as this will result in an even, vertical wall. If the clay starts to flare outward, you're pressing your thumb too hard on the inside. If the opposite occurs and the walls lean inward, then your fingers on the outside are pressing too hard. At this stage, don't thin the rim; that's best carried out later.

4 As the clay walls get thinner, you may feel like you're losing control of the form. It would be wise to let the piece stiffen by resting it rim-side down on the table. Once it's firmed up a little (but isn't leather hard!), the clay will be

more manageable and the walls can be pinched and thinned out even further. While the piece is resting, you could try your hand at making another.

5 In the final stages of thinning and shaping, you may find that you need to use your thumb more on the inside, stroking and pressing the clay to improve the regularity of the form [**D**]. Keep a close eye on the profile to make sure the walls are expanding evenly. If the rim seems too thick, you can thin it out with more pinches. For more about rim options, see page 23.

6 If your rim is noticeably uneven, trim it back using a potter's knife or some old scissors. Once your pot is almost leather hard, the irregularities in the surface can be scraped down with a hacksaw blade and smoothed out with a rubber rib. As with all craft techniques, the more you practice the technique, the more skilled you will become.

Pinching a Sphere

1 Begin with a smooth, round ball of clay (see first stage of Classic Pinch Pot, page 11). Once you've stuck your thumb into the clay ball, rotate the ball and pinch its lower three-quarters while leaving the clay toward the rim well alone; this thickness will be needed to create the uppermost inward curve. In the early stages of making a spherical form, the inside thumb does most of the shaping, while the fingers outside act as pressure absorbers, helping to support the clay and stop it from stretching too far. Remember, multiple small pinches yield better results than several large, forceful ones.

2 Once the lower curve is established, with the contour and thickness to your liking, the outside fingers take over the shaping. With your thumb on the inside and ready to steady and absorb pressure, pinch and slightly tug the clay

Supports: The Nest

There are several instances in which I recommend you support work in progress using a "nest." This is a simple, homemade apparatus that'll help in the construction of many pieces by preventing the base of your pot from flattening. Fill a plastic bag with fine sand, tie a knot, and place the bag in a sturdy flower pot or similar vessel. The bag of sand should be loosely packed and sit below the rim of the pot. Make a scooped impression in the sand and rest your pinch pot in it, making sure it's snug and secure.

inward. Remember to turn, turn, turn the form. I use my first two fingers on the outside, but you may prefer just your index finger—do whatever feels comfortable; there is no right or wrong way [E]. If at any time the pot begins to feel too soft and unmanageable, set it rim-side down to firm up a little.

3 With sufficient clay around the rim and with consistent pinching inwards toward the center, the form's opening can be made quite small. Study the contours and profile. You can continue to enlarge the fullness of the form and perfect its contours by using the pad of your index finger inside the "belly" and mouth of the pot. Stroke and gently push the clay, coaxing the curve outward. To keep the base from flattening while the pot is at rest or drying, sit the piece in a nest of plastic or on a small sand bag (see Supports: The Nest). An uneven rim, if not pleasing, can be trimmed with a knife or scissors.

A Wide Bowl

1 Prepare a small ball of clay and flatten it just a little by pressing the ball between your palms. The flattening should be just slight enough to make the ball not a true sphere.

2 Push the pad of your thumb down into the center, leaving at least ¼ inch (6 mm) of clay at the bottom. Remember, this is still a two-handed operation. You should be holding the clay, supporting it in the palm of your other hand.

3 Start the slow, pinching action, pressing harder this time with your inside thumb [F]. Press outward as you rotate, working from the base and spiraling upward.

The outside fingers, joined together like a paddle, aren't completely redundant; they help support the form and control its overall contour. Without your outside fingers in place, your bowl will end up a plate. It's most likely that you'll need to stop and let the clay firm up. Wide, hollow shapes are less stable when they're soft, so larger ones may need to be rested more often.

4 To safely lay this form down so it doesn't become misshapen, hold it rim-side up in your palm, lay a wooden board on the rim, and then flip the whole thing over with your hand still supporting the clay. It's a bit like turning a cake out of a pan!

5 As soon as the clay feels stiffer (but still has some give), lift the board and, while holding the clay, flip the clay back into your hand. Continue pinching as before, keeping a close eye on the profile to make sure you're not getting too wide. As always, work on the rim last. It will already have stretched and thinned out significantly. To thin it further, pinch the rim gently between thumb and index finger while slowly turning the form.

The Trumpet Shape

1 To make a tapered or flared form, prepare the clay as you would to make a cylinder (page 19), but after penetrating with your finger, pinch and stretch only one end. The thumb or finger pressing on the inside should exert the most pressure, forcing the clay in gradual stages to grow outwards [G]. Remember, in order to keep the shape regular, turn the clay slowly and frequently. There is no virtue in rushing! The other end can be worked to a greater or lesser extent, creating a double-trumpet effect.

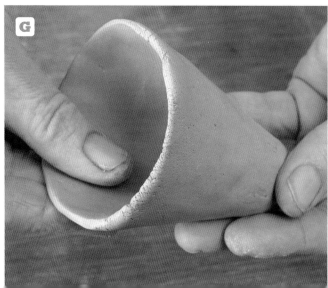

Incorporating a Neck

With this method, the neck evolves from the pot itself rather than being created and then added on separately. Incorporating the neck is a useful way of working with shapes that don't require a really long neck, and is especially good for small, delicate forms with which the process of adding on a neck could be too cumbersome. Some of the projects combine this type of neck with a lid, making this variation a valuable addition to your repertoire.

1   Begin by pinching a spherical form, as previously described on page 12. Keep the clay thick and chunky at the rim; more clay here will give you a taller neck. Make sure to plan ahead and know the size of the opening and the height of the neck.

2   When you've reached the point where the neck will begin, put your thumb on the inside of the piece and one or two fingers on the outside to bring the clay up. The first action is more of a flaring out; do this to the entire opening, then start pinching to give the form thinness and height. Even pressure with slight, upward tugs will heighten the walls and keep them straight. As with all outward curves, more pressure from the inside thumb or fingers will cause the clay wall to flare [H]. An inward lean needs more pressure from the outside fingers. These directional influences should be slow and rhythmic so you don't lose control of the form.

3   If the rim is too uneven or too long, trim it back with a sharp knife or scissors. If the clay is still very soft, let it rest until it's firm enough to handle without being distorted.

Composite Forms

There are other ways of making larger, more complex forms. The simple act of joining two or more shapes together allows the potter to really exploit the potential of the pinch technique, broadening the scope of design and function with endless, exciting possibilities. In terms of content, I feel that it rivals the wheel!

Join two bowls, and they become a sphere; two deep bowls, an egg shape; two plates, a flying saucer. Any of these shapes could be the foundation for a teapot, container, vase, or shaker set. You need not, however, restrict yourself to shapes that are similar. United, a cone and a saucer become a wonderful teardrop shape; a sphere and a cone, a club. The key to success is keeping the circumferences of the two joining edges the same; they must sit rim to rim if they're going to hold together and stay together. It's beneficial if the two shapes are of similar thickness. If one overhangs, you'll have to devote time to trimming back the excess, and the imbalance in weight could also affect the overall stability of the piece. The following instructions are intended for large- and small-scale work and for the joining of both similar and dissimilar forms.

1   If you're joining two similar shapes, you want each lump of clay to be as close in weight as possible. If you don't have a pair of scales, simply gauge the weight of each lump in your hands. Start shaping and pinching the first lump of clay, and, as soon as it begins to take shape, put it rim-side down on a piece of plastic so the rim doesn't dry out. Then pinch the second ball of clay, bringing it to about the same stage as the first.

2   Continue working back and forth between the two shapes; they should evolve simultaneously. It's imperative that every few minutes you hold them rim-to-rim to make sure their circumferences are similar. Don't let one lag behind, for it's much easier to bring them up together. Be alert as to the thickness of these rims. Pinch them too thin and joining them will be impossible, too chunky and the clay will be too thick. One-half inch (1.3 cm) of clay should be ample for a shape about the size of a football, less for smaller shapes. If your two halves become unmanageable and floppy, let them rest, rim sides down, on plastic. The halves shouldn't become leather hard, but rather just firm enough to better hold their shape [I].

3   Join the shapes when you're satisfied that the circumferences match, that the thicknesses are good, and that the clay is firm enough to handle. Check that the two joining edges are level. Unevenness will make life difficult, so trim back any unwanted clay. Using a toothbrush dipped in your

Joining with Slip

Slip is the potter's equivalent of glue. Whenever joining two clay elements, you must fix them together with slip—no matter the size, shape, or firmness. Even if the clay seems very soft, the addition of slip will make a stronger bond.

You can make slip by mixing bone-dry clay with water until it forms a thick, yogurt-smooth, homogenous liquid. You must always use slip that's made from the same clay as your pot. Apply it to the two joining areas using a stiff-bristled brush such as a toothbrush. Work the brush back and forth so that, as you deposit the slip, the surface of the clay roughens. Don't overload the joins with slip, for it will ooze out when the two parts are joined and make an unnecessary mess.

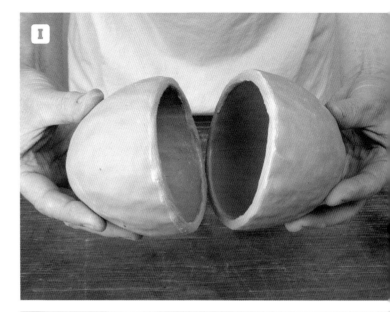

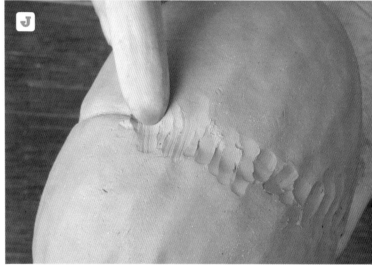

joining slip, brush and scratch the surface of both rims so that you give them a good coating of slip combined with a bit of roughness to the clay underneath. Don't overdo the slip—you don't want it running down the sides! Both forms should be firm enough to hold their own shape, so you can rest one on its side while you see to slipping the other.

4   Bring the two halves together, lining up the rims carefully. Press them firmly together and give one half a slight twist—you should feel it lock in, creating a strong bond. Now reinforce that join by running a wooden tool or your finger around the seam in a crisscross action as if you're stitching the shape together. Drag clay down over the seam and onto the other half. Alternate this action around the entire join [J]. The shape should now feel strong and sealed.

5   To disguise the join around the middle, roll out a soft coil of clay, flatten it slightly, and press it into the seam [K]. Use firm pressure, pressing the clay from behind as if chasing it around the pot. This way you won't trap any air.

6   Use your fingertips to smooth in the coil [L]. There should be no evidence that this shape was once two halves. It's worth noting that a sealed hollow form is a very strong one, even when the clay is soft. The air trapped inside

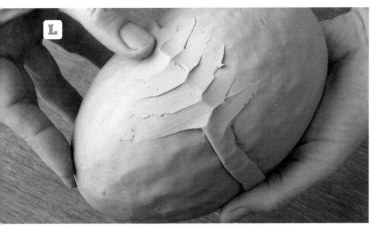

acts like an internal armature, holding up the form. It's rather like when you take a deep breath of air and hold it in. Take advantage of this strength: flatten the sides of the pot between your hands, create facets by beating it with a paddle, make a big dimple (or several), or press in tools to make textures or patterns.

7 When it's leather hard you can scrape and smooth the surface [M]. This is an excellent time to add a neck, feet, or handles. Before the form is too dry, it must be pierced open. All trapped air must have an exit before firing.

Creating a Disk

A disk is a useful shape for closing off the end(s) of an open form. It makes a good lid, and can easily be adapted to become a plate or saucer. There will be a lot of stretching at the rim, so, to avoid cracking, it's important to use very soft clay that's in good condition.

1 Gently flatten a ball of clay between your palms [N].

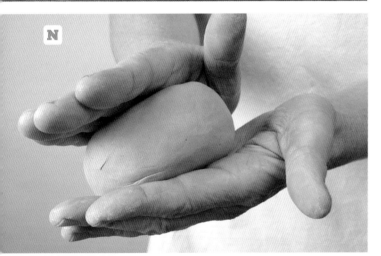

2 Press the pad of your thumb into the center. With your thumb working on the inside and fingers supporting the outside, rotate and press from the middle of the disk, working in a spiral toward the outside edge but keeping the rim fairly plump. If the clay is to stay relatively flat, the pressure from the thumb action on the inside should be significantly greater than that of the outside fingers [O].

3 In order to keep control of this wide, floppy shape, rest the clay intermittently. Cover the rim with plastic, allowing the main shape to firm up. As you continue working and the shape grows, focus your pinching on the center area, bringing this to the correct thickness before moving out toward the edge. This is especially important for larger shapes because, at some point, the disk may exceed the length of your thumb and forefinger, making the disk impossible to pinch. With patience it's possible to create very fine, thin pieces that require little or no scraping.

Something Larger

Generally, pinch pots are thought of as intimate, hand-sized pieces of pottery. However, there's a technique—a rather gutsy one—that allows you to make pieces of size and stature. There's more slapping than pinching involved, but the theory behind the technique is consistent with all that we've covered so far. This way of working is physically more demanding. You must approach the clay with intention: Make a commitment to the intended shape and stick to it. This technique is good for tall vase forms, rounded planters, or any large vessels that require height. Multiple, differing shapes can be joined together, opening up a whole new field of discovery.

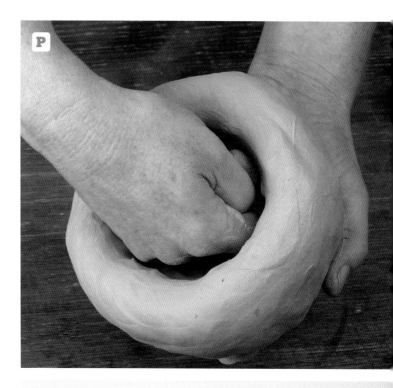

1   A large lump of clay, weighing about five pounds (roughly the size of a small melon), is a good starting point. Round the lump off in the usual way. Open up the center using your thumb, leaving a good thickness at the base and rim. Pinch the opening wide enough that you can get your fist in [P].

2   Tuck the thumb of your fisted hand inside your fingers to create a more uniform shape for the clay to rest on. Keeping your fist inside the clay, raise your arm vertically and begin slapping the outside of the form with your other hand. This hand, with its fingers joined together, acts like a paddle or beater. Each slap should be of equal energy as you work your way around the form. The slap should have a slight downward drag to it as it hits the clay, forcing the clay to grow down your arm like the beginning of a sleeve. Turn the clay after each slap, twisting your arm around clockwise as far as it will go and then shuffling your fist inside to move the clay around further. Don't neglect any one area because you can't reach it [Q]!

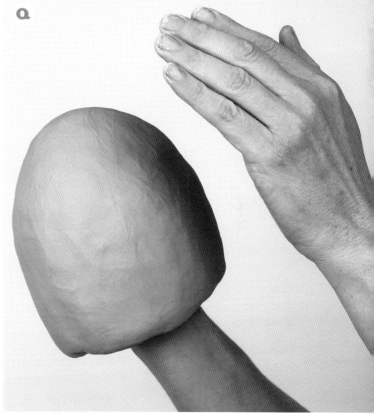

3   Keep your slapping movements away from the rim and from the very top portion of the clay, which covers your fist and will become the base. The thickness at the top is acting as much-needed support and can be thinned out later. To bring the walls up straight and even, it's important to keep your arm vertical. Start each slap from the upper sides of the clay, working your way down toward your elbow. I find at this stage that I tend to slap using my palm more than my fingers. Rotate the form just a little after each wave of slapping (from top to bottom) is complete. It's okay to take a break if your arm starts to ache. Carefully remove your fist and sit the clay shape on its rim; it should be thick enough to support its own weight. Don't let the clay dry out too much. If you think this is a danger, wrap the entire piece in plastic.

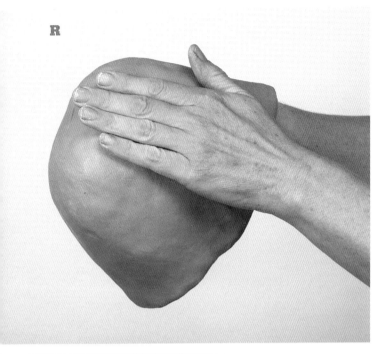

R

S

4 If you're interested in making a wider form, keep your arm at a more horizontal angle as you're slapping and shaping **[R]**. The pull of gravity will naturally open up the shape without you having to push from inside. Wider forms, being less self-supporting as they're made, may need more resting. Allowing the clay to firm up after every few inches of growth will enable you to keep better control of the form. Each time you rest the shape, place it rim-side down. As soon as the base and sides are firm enough to hold their own shape, you should rest the piece using the nest technique (page 12).

5 Whether making a wider or taller form, the piece can be removed from your arm as soon as the desired height is reached. You should be able to sit the piece in your lap or in the sandbag nest without it becoming misshapen. If it's not ready, let it dry out a little. Refining the form can now be done from the inside. To make the form swell out, stroke your joined fingers along the inside **[S]**. Sometimes, to correct the line of the profile, all that's needed is a few choice pushes of your fingertips on the inside.

6 Unless you're closing up the form so narrowly that you can't get your hand in, you should now finish the rim. Pinch it up between thumb and fingers to make it taller and thinner. Bring the rim inward by pressing and pulling the outside clay toward the middle, your thumb supporting the wall on the inside, or, if you prefer, thumb on the outside, fingers on the inside.

7 I encourage you to finish the base last. Thinning out this zone too soon can cause enough weakness in the structure of the pot that it collapses. Resting the pot in your lap makes it easier to finish the base. An old cushion or towel resting across your legs for extra cushioning would be a good idea. Support the clay in the cupped palm of one hand while the other goes to work inside. Thumb, fingertips, knuckles— use whatever feels like the best tool for pressing out the remaining clay. You don't have to work it to paper thinness; the bases on most pots are generally thicker than on the sides. Keep a vigilant eye on the overall form, turning and holding up the pot regularly to check its sides and profile.

OPEN-ENDED SHAPES

Open-ended forms are an invaluable addition to the pinch repertoire, helping you expand functional possibilities while offering the opportunity to play with overall aesthetics. Pouring spouts, necks, handles, lugs, feet, and stems for bowls can all be made using this simple method. All the shapes suggested can be cut and modified, or sliced into sections at the leather-hard stage.

Simple Cylindrical Forms

The cylinder is a valuable asset to the basic shape group. Whether short or long, wide or narrow, it can add width and height to a form—or be the form itself! Remember, not all pinch pots have to be spherical. Cylindrical forms can become necks or pedestal-like feet. Scaled down you could make a simple spout or slice one up like a loaf of bread to make hoops for a raised surface design.

1 Round off a ball of clay in your hands. The amount will depend on what you're making—you will most likely need to repeat this process a few times before you get the right width and length, but trial and error is all part of the process! When you have a nice smooth ball, roll and pat it in both hands to make it more log-shaped. Aim to keep the sides parallel. Carefully and slowly stick your thumb or little finger (or pencil if it is a small piece of clay) down the center of its length until it emerges through the other side.

2 Smooth down the edges of the clay that are torn and thin—this will be at the far end where your finger/stick has burst through.

3 With your thumb inside and index finger outside (or whatever combination of fingers works best), begin pinching and turning the clay with an even pressure. You may find that a pinch-tug is necessary to help the shape stretch and grow in length.

4 Flip the shape around and work the other end in exactly the same way [A]. Work back and forth between both ends to create a neat cylindrical form. Large versions of this shape may need to sit and rest, allowing the clay to dry out and firm up before moving on. When leather hard, the tube can be cut into smaller lengths or angular-ended tubes.

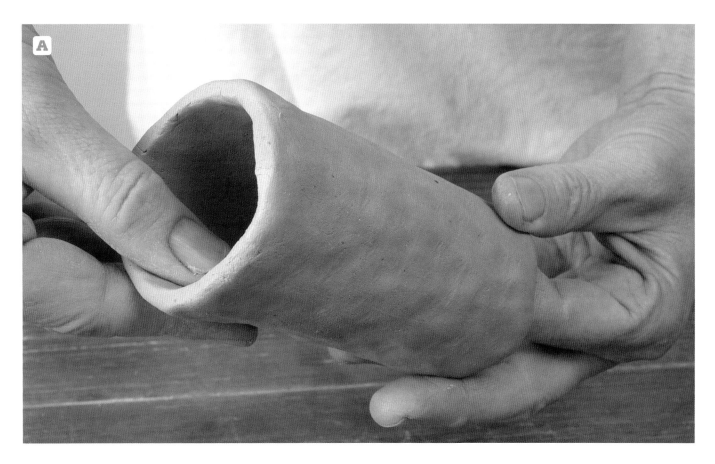

A

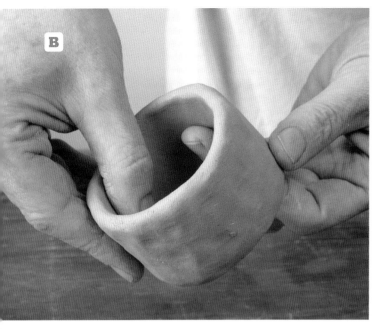

Barrel, Collar, & Spherical Shapes

All of these shapes are useful additions to your repertoire. If scaled up, they can become the basis for a main body shape, such as a teapot or a mug. If scaled down, they are invaluable as elements for a neck or a foot.

1 Prepare the clay as for making a cylinder, adjusting the length of the "log" according to need.

2 When you get to the stage where you've pierced through the form, use either your thumb or index finger (whatever works) and begin to coax the clay out from around its middle. Stroke the pad of one finger from the inside toward the opening, easing off the pressure as you go. Turn the clay just a fraction after each move and remember to work from both ends, going back and forth continually. If making a wide collar, pinch with equal pressure from both ends [B]. Your outside fingers or thumb should be assisting, ready to counteract the pressure coming from within. The more you stretch the clay the thinner it'll become, so make sure you have sufficient thickness for what you intend to make.

3 If making a very spherical form [C], you'll need to apply more continued pressure on the inside, especially at the center [D]. Ease off the pressure gradually. As you press from the center toward the opening, gradually lessen the pressure so that you're barely touching the opening.

4 Work from both ends of the shape, going back and forth as the shape begins to swell and grow. Continually check the profile of the curve and don't forget to let it dry out if it starts to become unmanageable.

Spouts & Tapered Tubes

The tapered tube, that seemingly inconsequential form, is the foundation shape for making pouring spouts.

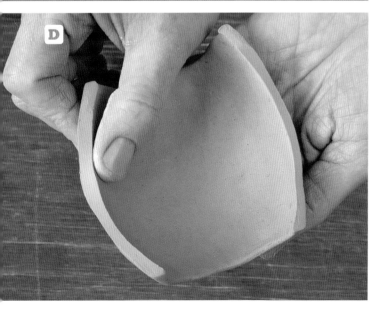

1 To make a small tapered tube you'll have to employ the use of a pencil. Begin by rounding off a soft ball of clay, then patting it in both hands to make it more log-shaped. Taper the log somewhat by patting, rolling, or pinching one end. Keep all the edges slightly rounded; this stops them from getting thin and tearing.

2 Starting at the wider end, push your finger or a pencil through the center of the clay (use a stick or dowel for larger shapes). Only go all the way through if you intend to make a spout or tube shape [E].

3 Start pinching at the wider open end. If the hole is too small for your fingers, put the pencil back in and wiggle it in circles to open up the space. Unless the shape is large, you'll be pinching with just the first joint of your thumb and index finger. Pinch and rotate with a little more pressure from inside; this will widen the form [F].

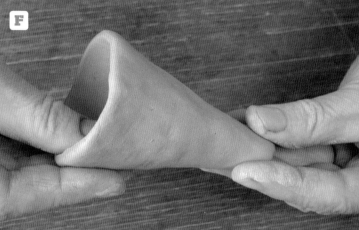

4 Work on the opposite narrower end—you may need to wiggle and rotate a pencil inside to make the opening wider. For large spouts, you should be able to get your fingertips inside to help with the forming. For more delicate spouts, leave the pencil in and gently squeeze the clay around it. A variation would be to cup and squeeze the clay in the palm of one hand, rotating after every movement. Be careful not to close up the inside channel! Swivel the pencil from time to time to make sure the clay isn't sticking. The idea at this stage is to thin and lengthen the narrower end.

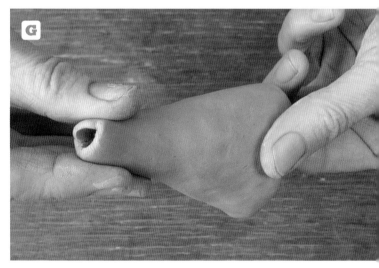

5 Remove the pencil and continue to shape the form at both ends. You can further narrow the pointy end by gently pulling the clay between your fingers while your other hand rotates and tugs [G]. These are all small but deliberate movements made as you stretch the clay.

6 For a teapot spout, one end should be wider than the other (usually the wider part fixes to the body of the teapot). To give the spout flowing contours, push out the curves from inside with a gentle wiping movement of your fingertip or the end of a soft paintbrush [H]. Areas that need to curve inwards can be carefully pressed and coaxed from the outside. Don't try and make the spout all in one go—letting it firm up after some basic shaping will allow for more control. I often make two or three spouts at the same time, knowing that perhaps only one of them will be just right. The chosen spout must be fitted and trimmed in several stages by you holding it up to the teapot body and making the necessary alterations, working rather like a tailor. Once the spout is slipped and joined to the pot, you can refine it further by shaving and trimming it with various modeling tools.

ADDING ELEMENTS TO YOUR FORM

All of the following elements add interest and extend the functionality of your pots. For example, lips and feet may be considered minor pieces of information, but they can have a staggering influence over the personality of your piece. With the addition of a lid, a cylinder can become a covered jar.

LIPS & EDGES

Rim, lip, brim—these terms refer to the edge of a pot, that area of transition where the outside and inside of a form meet. This seemingly insignificant part of a pot's anatomy is often overlooked or neglected and must be thought through from the start. No matter how great the pot or how strong the proportion, pattern, or color, if the rim is scruffy and neglected, it'll detract from the overall appearance.

The rim must be considered at the pot's very conception. If it's not, the rim will not only look like an afterthought, weak and unsure of itself, but you may not have left enough clay to make the design statement that you suddenly envision. It's as vital a design aspect as a handle, foot, or lid, and so must be given equal consideration. There are dozens of options to consider. Look at any vessel in any material and you'll see rims in a variety of shapes, sizes, and thicknesses. Some are quite decorative; others are large and make a bold statement. More often than not, and especially in the case of drinking vessels, a simple smooth, thin edge is all that's required to make a satisfying finish. Unless deliberately designed, sharp and ragged edges can be displeasing and should be avoided for utilitarian ware. Smooth, rounder edges are not only more tactile and inviting but less likely to chip. Study objects in the natural world—the edges of leaves and shells, the rhythmic order of petals and buds—and harvest from them clues and solutions for your work.

A very thin lip can give the illusion of a lightweight pot, while a thick lip will imbue the form with a heavy, more solid quality. Rims can be highly decorative or plain and simple. Between these extremes there are many individual variations to explore. Here's a selection of ideas to whet your appetite and get you started. Consider the practical needs of your pot as well as its character, and design the lip accordingly.

Some points to remember:
»» Level the top of the pinch pot before shaping or adding to the rim. Do this by holding the pot at eye level and trimming off the high areas with a sharp knife, scissors, or needle.
»» If the clay is too dry, pinching and shaping the rim will cause it to crack and split. This can be exploited for a decorative effect.
»» Let the piece rest and firm up. This will give you more control over shape and thickness. Don't try and do it all in one go.
»» All cut edges can be softened with the tip of a finger dipped in water.
»» The rim isn't exclusive to a bowl or a mug; it's the fitting around a lid and the edge of the lid itself. No matter what the vessel, it's the place where inside and outside converge.

SCALLOP RIM

RIPPLE EDGE

FRAYED EDGE

CUT EDGE

PIERCED EDGE

A Simple, Thin Lip— Spare & Elegant

The pinching and thinning of the rim should be addressed only when the main pot shape has been established. While the clay is still soft, equal pinching pressure between your thumb and index finger is sufficient to thin the rim [A]. Any inward or outward tilt to the rim must be made before the clay gets too firm, as then the rim becomes difficult to pinch and unwanted splitting may occur. If you don't want a wavy, undulating edge, trim the rim level before it gets too thin. Now is the time to use a hacksaw blade or similar tool to shave away unwanted clay.

A Thicker Rim—A Couple of Ways to Get One

The simplest method for creating a thick rim is to not pinch the rim at all until you've finished shaping the pot. When you're ready to deal with the rim, it should first be trimmed level, then turned outward or inward, or left straight. You can further define the rim by pinching just below it, not so much thinning the clay as making a more distinct separation between the rim and the wall of the pot.

A second option for a thick rim is to add a coil [B]. This method is very versatile and will allow for more control and variation. The soft coil can be added to any part of the rim, but be sure that you firmly attach it and then smooth in all the seams. Once joined, the coil can be flattened, bent, folded, crimped, textured, and patterned.

A Ripple Edge— Endless Options

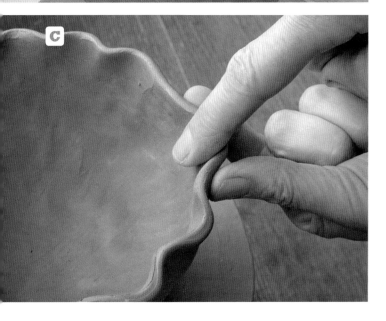

There are many variations on this piecrust effect, but all of them must be carried out when the clay is still very flexible. Adding a soft coil onto the pot is an option, but very often the lip of the original pot is still malleable enough to work with. Results will differ depending upon the thickness of the clay.

A traditional wavy edge, sometimes seen on flowerpots, is achieved by pulling the clay rim outward with the swift tug of a finger. The thumb and index finger of one of your hands are placed slightly apart on the outside of the rim. From inside, push the clay into the space using the thumb or finger of your other hand. The rhythm and pressure applied must be steady and even as the pot is rotated. The bigger the gap between the outside fingers, the bigger the ripple [C].

A more scalloped effect can be achieved by pressing down on the top or side of the soft rim with the side of a dowel or thumb. All sorts of pinching, crimping, and pressing actions—done with the ends and sides of sticks, forks, spoons, and the like—can be carried out to create a decorative edge.

A Frayed Edge— Impactful if Intentional

The cracking of the rim that I continually forewarn you against can be harnessed and utilized to decorative effect, but it's best suited for less utilitarian, more sculptural pieces. For it to have the intended effect, it should be controlled and considered, otherwise there's a good chance it'll look weak and accidental.

After shaping, allow the pot to firm up. Keeping the rim a little thicker will allow for more emphatic splitting as the clay is stretched out further. The dryer the edge, the more it'll split. For a more sculptural effect, the rim could be made to undulate, further emphasizing the organic qualities of the piece. See [D].

Cut Edges—Clean & Neat

Cutting the rim when it's leather hard offers tremendous opportunity for creating decorative and sculptural edges. This technique can also be adapted for use on feet and lids. Having the correct tools for the job is vital. Cuts need to be clean and precise, so a sharp knife is essential.

Planning out even the simplest design is a necessary part of the process. Failure to do this can cause an irregular series of cuts with inconsistent spacing. Working with a paper template or sketching out your design on the pot first will allow you to lay out the design correctly and concentrate on the cutting. Use a wet finger to smooth out any harsh, cut edges.

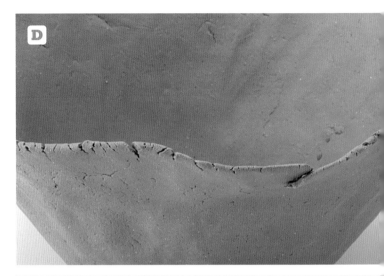

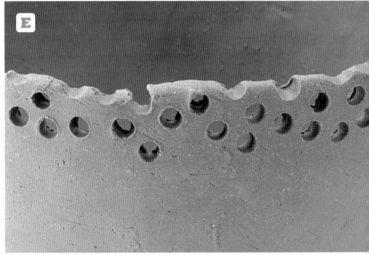

Piercing—Using Negative Space as a Design Element

This technique is a purely decorative way of altering the rim of a pot—one you might use for a bowl or a planter rather than a mug. Various shapes and designs are cut out of the leather-hard clay to create negative space. It's critical to use a sharp, thin blade in order to make precise cuts. A hole-making tool (they are sold in several gauge sizes) can also be used to create interesting effects (as seen in [E]). It is possible to cut through any type of clay, but the results are more successful with smooth ungrogged bodies.

FEET & FOOT RINGS

There is no rule that a pot has to have a foot ring or feet; a flat base is perfectly sufficient. However, the addition of a built-on foot offers the exciting opportunity to play with aesthetics. No matter the size of a pot, form, function, and proportion will be affected by the addition of feet.

For very little effort, inclusion of a tall foot will naturally increase the size of your piece, thereby amplifying the sense of drama, too! But feet can also be subtle, creating a quiet lift to the form. Even the smallest elevation can change the entire perception of a piece.

There are inverted feet, which are only visible when the pot is turned over and appear as hollowed-out rings or dimples. This feature is more properly called a foot ring. Look at the bowls and cups in your kitchen; they're likely to have this kind of detail.

Whatever kind you choose, feet are best added when the pot is leather hard. Always use the same clay as the pot for your feet and for the joining slip. Employ a banding wheel when you're no longer manipulating the piece in your hands. Continued finishing of the foot ring can be carried out when the clay has become leather hard—just be sure to wrap the main body of the pot in plastic while the foot is firming up.

Here I've proposed a selection of simple feet that you might like to try. Naturally, the scale and proportion can be adapted to suit your needs. Some shapes, such as the bowl and the trumpet, can be combined to make more complex foot combinations in which the foot becomes more a pedestal. Pierced, textured, or carved, the edges of these feet are finished in the same way as rims—the potential is enormous. I hope you'll continue to investigate the possibilities.

DOUGHNUT FOOT

COILED FOOT RING

NODULE FEET

POD FEET

TALL FOOT

PINCHED BOWL FOOT

PUSHED OUT FOOT

A Simple Coiled Foot Ring— Elegant & Understated

1 Once your pot is almost leather hard, roll a very soft coil of clay as long, at least, as the diameter of the bottom of your pot. Place the coil onto the base of your pot in a circle [A], marking off its position with a pencil or stick.

2 Add slip to the marked area, and, in an all-in-one movement, press in the coil from the sides while forcing it gently downward. This will straighten the sides and stop the coil from becoming overly squashed.

3 Trim off the end of the coil, blending the clay in where the two ends meet.

4 Thumb the outside of the coil downward onto the pot, easing and blending it in [B]. Use a wooden tool if it's easier. Decide if you want the foot taller, shorter, curving outwards, or inwards, and adjust the profile as necessary. Stand the pot up to check its balance and overall appearance. Trim off any unwanted clay, making sure to smooth the cut edge.

The Doughnut Foot— Plump & Pneumatic

1 Pinch a fairly thick, soft bowl.

2 Position the bowl on the bottom of the pot and mark the joining area with a pencil [C].

3 Add slip to the pot and gently press the bowl into place, being careful not to dent the middle. Smooth in the clay around the join—the bowl should now look like a bulge [D].

4 With the fleshy pad of your thumb, begin to press in the center of the freshly joined bulge using small rhythmic movements [E]. One violent press and the bulge may pop. Rotate the form while you continue shaping. You should only need to work the inside of the foot. Aim for a neat, circular depression. The outside rim should look full and inflated.

5 Stand the vessel up, supporting it while you check that it's level. To release the trapped air, use a needle tool to pierce the base of the foot ring when it's leather hard.

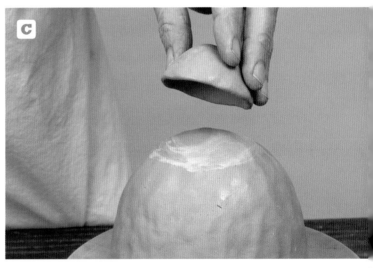

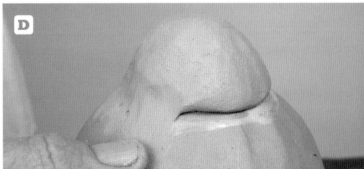

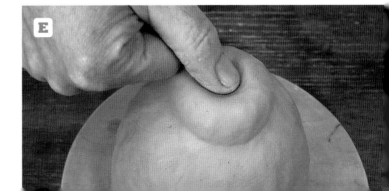

Nodule Feet—
Eye-Catching Yet Organic

The method is the same regardless of the number of feet.

1   Pinch off three equal-sized lumps of clay and roll them into balls.

2   Use a pencil to mark off the places on the base of the pot where they are to be joined, checking that they're equally spaced for stability.

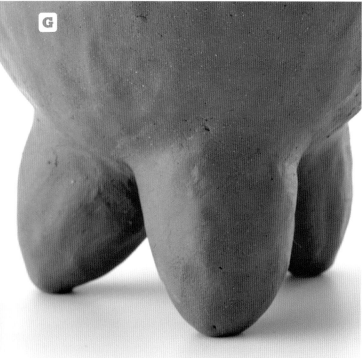

3   Slip the contact area and press the balls into place. Ease the clay around each ball down onto the pot and smooth it in. A damp finger is a good tool for smoothing and shaping each nodule. For visual strength, the thickest part should be where the foot grows out of the pot. Support the pot in your hands while you establish the balance and check the level [F].

TIP: For longer feet, increase the amount of clay, and, instead of making the clay into ball shapes, roll it into a coil and then cut it into equal lengths. Affix the lengths in the same way as described above, making sure not to over thin the area at the join. If desired, you can carve and shape the feet as they become leather hard.

Pod Feet—Sturdy & Bold

1   Round off three or more lumps of clay and start pinching as if you were making mini pinch pots. The lumps can be shallow and round or long and torpedo shaped. Pinch with the appropriate pressure to get the result you want.

2   You have two choices as to when to join the feet to the pot: now, while they're still soft, or later, when they're firmer. It's a personal choice. I like to join the feet while they're still relatively soft, as this allows me to manipulate the shapes as well as their angles in order to get a well-balanced result. Either way, select and mark with a pencil the position of each foot.

3   You may find it helpful to trim the opening of each foot at a slight curve that corresponds to the angle of the pot. Slip and then join, thumbing in the clay at the seam. In this case, a flared edge on the rim of each foot will allow for better joining [G].

NOTE: Don't forget that these are hollow shapes and at some stage in the drying must have a needle poked through them to allow the air to escape.

A Tall Foot—
For Dramatic Elevation

Make a tall foot from an open-ended tube. It'll be trial and error as to how much clay you'll need.

1 Pat the clay into a round-ended log.

2 Press a thumb or finger into one of the ends to create an opening. If it doesn't go all the way through, pierce through the other end with a finger.

3 I tend to start pinching the widest end first, but there's no rule. Work back and forth between the ends, checking the overall proportion by holding the foot up to the vessel. If creating a very large piece, you can let the foot dry separately until it's almost leather hard; this may make it easier to join.

4 Slip both parts before assembling and use a soft coil of clay to reinforce the seam.

Pinched Bowl Foot—
A Sturdy Pedestal

1 Make a pinch bowl. From the beginning, have in mind the size and shape of the bowl intended. Do you envision it deep and tall, or shallow and wide? Gauging the amount of clay needed will be a case of trial and error. Use your first attempt as a guide.

2 Trim the edge of the foot if it is very uneven. When you're satisfied with the shape, flip it over and join it, bump to bump, so to speak, with slip to the base of your pot. If the pot's base is very rounded, you may want to shave it down to something flatter, giving it a greater contact area. This will help in the joining. Press the two shapes together from the insides of the pots. Be gentle but firm.

3 Stand the pot up to check that it's level and stable.

4 Unite the two shapes further by pressing a soft coil of clay into the outside join, thumbing in the clay to the pot and down onto the new foot. Further finishing can be carried out when the foot has become leather hard [H].

Pushed-In Foot—
Quick & Simple

1 Pinch and shape your pot, making sure to leave some thickness at the base. Allow the shape to firm up just a little; the clay needs to be soft but not wobbly.

2 Press the pad of your thumb or index finger into the center of the base, using a gentle, circular motion, as if cleaning a window. Slowly rotate the pot as the depression widens and deepens; it should start to look like a small bowl. Dampen your finger if it keeps dragging, but don't let the clay get soggy. Keep a check on how much you're stretching the clay—you don't want to burst through to the inside!

3 Inside, you'll see a hump in the bottom. Don't fiddle with it. Any interference and it will lose its fresh, organic quality. This inner bump can be an interesting feature in bowl and cup designs. Stand the pot up and carefully correct the level of the new foot ring by patting the base gently on the table.

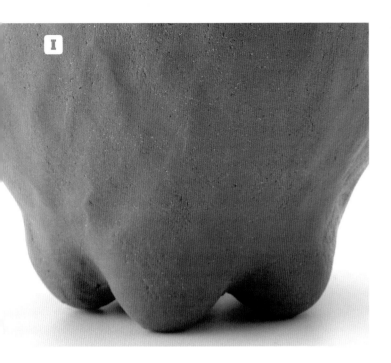

Pushed Out Feet—
An Animalistic Quality

1 This is an all-in-one method to be carried out when the clay vessel has just been formed and is still very soft. Start pinching the pot shape, keeping the base nice and chunky. The bigger the foot bumps, the more clay you will need in reserve.

2 As the pot takes shape, start to incorporate the feet. For small bumps, use the pad of a finger, pressing it gently into the base from inside. Let the bumpy feet grow and evolve simultaneously.

3 As the clay firms up (particularly the main body of the vessel), you can go back in and push a little more. Wiggling your finger in each depression will enlarge the bump. Aim to keep each bump a similar height to help with stability. For really big bumps, you'll need to work more slowly and carefully in order to keep control of each shape and the form's overall rhythm. Use the pad of your thumb, stroking and teasing out the clay from inside to create the swellings. Eventually, it might be easier to use several fingers together. Rest the pot if it becomes unmanageable; a little drying off time between working will allow you to keep control of the form [**I**].

HANDLES

The addition of a handle or handles to your pot opens up an exciting array of functional and decorative possibilities. Learning to make and attach handles requires some practice and patience. It's easy, especially at the joining stage, to over manipulate the clay, which may result in a tired and weak appendage. The handle should be seen as part of the overall pot and given as much attention as all other aspects. It must be made with conviction and be in balance with the entire pot. This isn't to say that all handles must be practical, but even as decorative elements, they should look intentional and be placed with purpose.

Decorative handles are often, though not exclusively, used more as an embellishment than out of necessity. There is a dynamic range of possibilities to choose from: loops, knuckle-like knobs of clay, daintily pinched ears, and large patterned fins that project like wings, to name a few. Large or small, applied singly or in multiples, handles can transform a vase or jar. Whether a handle makes a grand gesture or a small statement, its style, size, and placement must be as thoroughly considered as all other aspects of the piece. Many good examples can be found if you look at ceramic history, particularly Japanese and medieval pottery.

On bowls and jars, a pair of handles can serve a practical purpose, providing an easier, more balanced grip. This is especially useful on a wide bowl or ovenproof dish. A large, heavy jar equipped with two strap handles (traditionally called lugs), which are set horizontally on either side like a pair of ledges, will allow for a sturdy and safe lift.

A tapered handle gives the feeling of growth and strength. Traditionally, the thicker end starts at the top, but this isn't a rule that must be strictly adhered to.

Handles are generally positioned so that they bridge the concave part of the pot. This prevents them from over protruding and looking cumbersome. From a practical viewpoint, handles on mugs, jugs, and teapots should be designed so that there's room for the fingers to have a comfortable grip.

There are some general rules to bear in mind when creating handles:
➺ All of the handles that follow require soft clay. After being formed and shaped, they should be left to stiffen.
➺ To allow for trimming, always make handles longer than you need.
➺ It's vital that handle and pot are joined when the clay is at the same stage of dryness—ideally, this is shortly before leather hard.
➺ As with all attachments, it's necessary to roughen and slip the joining area.

COIL

STRAP

BRAIDED

PATTERNED FIN

Strap & Coil Handles— Workhorses of the Handle World

These handles are extremely versatile and can be maximized and minimized to suit many pot forms.

1 For the strap handle, roll a soft coil of clay so that it's smooth and even. Bear in mind that as it's flattened, it'll widen. Trying to gauge the exact diameter of the starting coil takes practice, so, to begin with, I suggest making several and keeping the best. For a tapered handle, you must taper the coil now by rolling one end thin; it should look like a very long carrot. Starting at one end, gently flatten the coil using the side or fleshy part of your hand (base of the thumb), pressing down the length with a steady pressure. You can also try laying a flat board on top and pressing

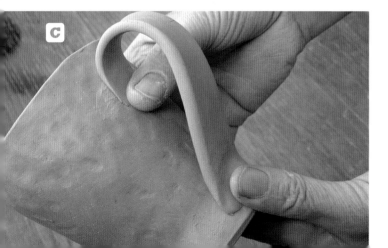

down. Either way, the flattening process should be done in stages so as not to over crush the shape. To taper thickness, increase the tapping pressure as you work your way from the thick end to the thin. If you want to press a texture into the handle, do it after this stage of shaping. A dowel laid down along the center length and pressed in can give a lovely raised edge to a strap handle [A].

2 Rolling and flattening a very fat coil can make a striking blade-like handle, like that of an ancient axe. This style of handle may not be the most practical due to its depth and small inner curve, so use it wisely! Set the shape of the curve before you compress it. Because of its broad, plain surface, you may like to explore some mark making.

3 Of course, you don't have to flatten the coil at all. A simple cord-like handle is worth exploring, too. Try a tapered version or a coil that's partially flattened at the ends or middle. See what exciting things happen when you roll it over a textured surface.

4 When you're satisfied with the width and thickness, cut off any obvious unwanted length, but leave a little to play with. Lay the handle on its side and carefully shape it so that it begins to flow into the kind of curve you want [B]. Hold the pot (in profile) close up and visualize the flow of the handle against the form, adjusting the handle's curve accordingly. Let it stiffen.

5 Once the handle can hold its shape, you can fit it to the pot. Mark off the two joining areas with a stick or other fairly pointy tool, checking from several angles that the areas line up. Sometimes a light vertical line sketched onto the pot can help with the placement. The joining ends may need an angular cut that corresponds to the profile of the pot. This will create a more energetic feel. A blunt cut, one joined at right angles, can look rigid and awkward. Usually the thicker end is joined first [C]. The lower end can be welded in the same way or pressed on as an overlap, the extra length trimmed away.

6 Once the handle is joined, try not to over-work it. There should be enough softness in the clay to allow you to adjust the curve. Study its appearance from both sides and from head on. Put some distance between you and the pot. Standing several feet away and scrutinizing its appearance can be a very useful exercise, as suddenly, weaknesses and design flaws become more apparent.

Braided Handle—Very Decorative

This handle was used frequently by potters in the 19th century. To make it successfully you'll need very soft plastic clay that won't crack with all the bending and twisting.

1 Roll out three coils of the same thickness. Tapered coils can be used if you want the handle to narrow or thin [D].

2 Lay the coils side by side so that they touch [E].

3 Press the coils together at one end (if using tapered coils, join the thicker ends) to act like a holding knot, then, with a coil in each hand, begin to braid, in a steady, continuous rhythm. Try to avoid gaps in the braiding [F].

4 You can flatten the braid to make it slimmer, but don't flatten it too much or you'll lose definition [G].

5 Another method is to twist two (or three) coils together, as if you were winding something up [H]. This will produce a more ropelike result. Flatten slightly if desired [I]. Begin the shaping and drying process as described previously.

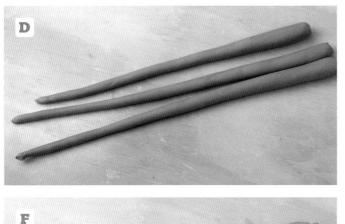

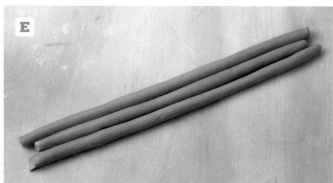

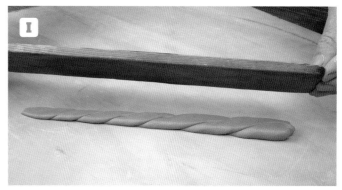

LIDS

The lid of your pot should be given as much design consideration as any other part of your pot. Pinched lids are very easy to make, and there are many different styles to choose from. Some are more practical than others. Understanding the basic idea behind each shape will help you decide which is most suited to your piece. For instance, a teapot that's intended to be used regularly should have a secure and snugly fitting lid, whereas a teapot that's intended more as a decorative object with only the occasional period of active service can afford a more frivolous style of lid.

A few key points to remember:

»» Don't start fitting lids or cutting open forms until the pot is strong enough to hold its own shape.

»» Invest in a pair of calipers—this is an invaluable tool that enables you to accurately measure and gauge the diameter of the lid and its opening.

»» Avoid making very tight-fitting lids. Clay often contracts unevenly and the lid will invariably get stuck in place during one of the kiln firings. The lid should fit snugly but still have some space to move. If it doesn't wiggle, it's too tight!

»» When possible, the lid and the lid fitting should be modeled when the clays are in the same state.

»» Knobs should be added after you've shaped and sized the lid.

»» Scratch and slip the joining areas of anything you add on.

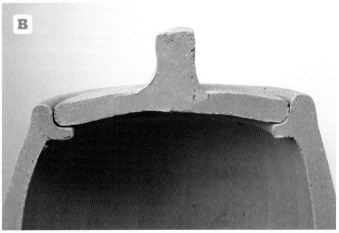

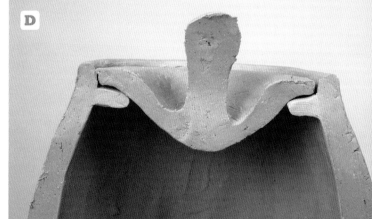

An Inset Dish Lid— The Simplest Lid to Make

This lid is nothing more than a pinched bowl or dish. It's a loose, inverted cover that sits concavely in the opening, or across the top of the opening where it rests on the lip of the pot [A].

FLAT INSET LID WITH A GALLERY

A simple pinched disk, trimmed when leather hard, that sits on the rim of a gallery fitting. A flange can be added to the underside of the lid for more security [B].

Sophisticated Dish Lid— Add a Gallery

The simple dish-shaped lid can be developed further by giving it a turned-out lip. This flat edge or rim sits over the top of the pot and prevents the pot from sliding out. For even more accuracy, a flange, or "gallery," can be built into the inside opening of the pot (photo [C]). The flange is simply a flattened coil of clay joined to the inside of the pot, creating a horizontal ledge and acting like a deep socket for the lid to sit in.

The lip on the lid should be turned out during the pinching and shaping stage, when the clay is still flexible. The turned out rim of the lid sits on the gallery, making it completely inset [D].

Convex Lid or Cover— A Bowl Inverted

Here is the simple bowl again, except that this time it's flipped over so that it projects out of the pot. There are two ways that it can sit in place. The first is to use it like a sleeve so that it covers the neck of your pot [E]. For this you may need to build on a vertical flange or neck to the opening of your pot.

The second option is to inset a flange into the inside rim of the lid itself—allowing it to sit rim to rim with the post, making a clean, uninterrupted flow of forms [F].

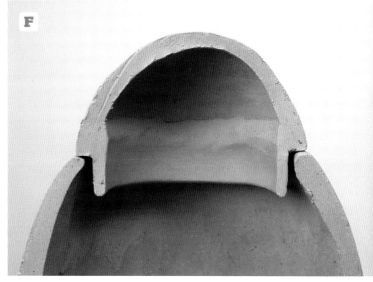

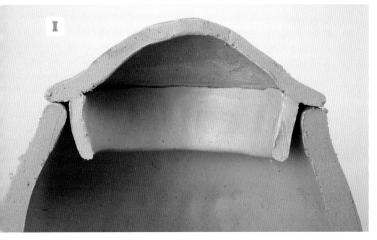

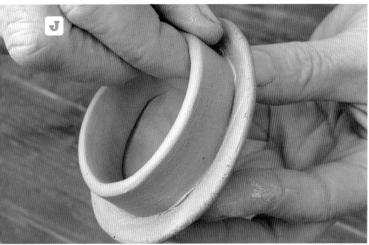

Pebble Pot Lid—
Part of the Pot Itself

This lid fitting is not made separately but rather cut and incorporated from the pot itself. It doesn't necessarily require a knob or handle, since the whole lid is designed to be removed in a grasp of the hand. It has great sculptural possibilities, but also has practical merits. The cutting line of the lid can be highly stylized and geometric, or it can have an organic flow and rhythm that echoes the form of the pot [G]. Whichever design you choose, it's likely that the lid will only fit back into position one way.

For a clean, accurate cut, work only when the piece is leather hard. Use a pencil to sketch the cutting line onto the clay. Use a ruler and a coin if you've selected the version that has notches, as you'll need three semicircular notches to keep the lid in place [H]. Use a sharp knife with a thin, stiff blade. To prevent warping, dry the form with the two parts in place.

Flanged Lid—
The Most Secure Lid

This might be the most involved and complex of all the lid fittings, but in terms of function, it's probably the most secure. The lid has a built-in flange, which should be quite generous and deep, that hangs down into the cavity of the vessel [I]. It can also be combined with a pot that has a gallery, making it more inset and even more secure. This is the kind of lid fitting you're likely to see on a traditional teapot.

When you're pinching your lid shape, leave some thickness at the rim. Let it firm up. Add on another flattened coil positioned at right angles to the inside lip of the lid. The circumference of this strip of clay must correspond to the circumference of the opening of the pot—if anything, make it a few millimeters narrower to allow for uneven shrinkage [J].

KNOBS

There are absolutely no rules when it comes to knobs! Large, small, pointy, round, thick, squeezed, flattened—the palette is infinite. You could even make a knob by affixing a found object—like a stick, rock, or metal cog—post firing. The style and size of knob (I'm talking strictly about the handle you put on a lid) will give your pot a certain personality. Large round knobs tend to lend a humorous tone, whereas a small pointed one has a more serious, restrained tone. Knobs need not be symmetrical. A soft squeezed lump of clay may be just the detail you're looking for, and it may look better

off center than on. Some knobs can be adapted strap or wing handles (see Handles, page 30). The only restraint I might impose is one of practicality. If your vessel has an intended function, particularly one that brings it into daily usage, consider the safety of the knob. Is it likely to chip because it's too long or detailed? Is it too cumbersome or too dainty in the hand to be practical? Unless the piece is purely decorative, these questions should underpin your design decisions. Other than that, though, enjoy exploring this expressive area of your pot.

BULBOUS

SPAGHETTI

COIL

COOKIE

STRAP

SPROUT

MARY E. ROGERS Born in 1929 in Belper, Derbyshire, England, Mary studied graphic design at Watford School of Art and St. Martin's School of Art. A growing interest in ceramics led her to continue her studies at Loughborough College of Art and Design and to set up a workshop in 1960 concentrating on handbuilt stoneware and porcelain. Around 1990, Mary was forced to give up working in ceramics for health reasons. She now works and exhibits as a painter and photographer. Her pieces are in the collections of major museums in Britain, the United States, Australia, New Zealand, Japan, Germany, Netherlands, Norway, Switzerland, and Belgium. She is the author of *Mary Rogers on Pottery and Porcelain: A Handbuilder's Approach*, a book about her sources of inspiration and methods of working.

A *PAPYRUS FOLDS*, 1983, 5½ x 4" (14 x 10.2 cm) approx   **B** *STRIATED CRINOID*, 1983, 5 x 4¾" (12.7 x 12.1 cm) approx
C *SKY BOWL*, 1981, 4" (10.2 cm) wide approx   **D** *SLICED AGATE*, 1983, 7" (17.8 cm) wide approx   **E** *CONVOLUTED BOWL*, 1971, 6" (15.2 cm) diameter approx   **F** *BEAKED BIRD*, 1985, 5" (12.7 cm) wide approx

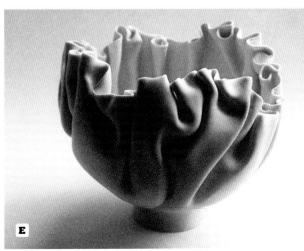

PRE-FIRED SURFACE TREATMENTS

The unfired clay surface is an exciting canvas for decorating, with many techniques to choose from. There are four basic approaches for altering the surface: A painterly approach involving slips or oxides, adding clay (as in relief surfaces), subtracting clay (as in carving and sgraffito), and lastly, impressing the clay. These techniques are not mutually exclusive, and in careful combination can be quite striking.

Part of your decision making—and this really is an aspect of design—must be to consider the purpose of the vessel and whether your surface treatment is appropriate to its usage. Does it hinder/obstruct functionality? Do what is right for the piece. The more ornamental your pot, the more unorthodox your decoration can be.

ADDING AND SUBTRACTING CLAY

Techniques for ceramic decoration need not be limited to slips and glazes. During the production stage, pattern can be created by use of texture, whether raised, incised, or impressed—it carries as much decorative potential as the painted surface, and, of course, they're not mutually exclusive.

All the following techniques are for treating the clay surface in its unfired state. Results will vary enormously depending on the softness/hardness of the clay and whether it is a smooth or groggy body. The techniques of stamping, carving, and joining are some of the earliest methods used to decorate pottery and are ones that continue to have great potential for the contemporary potter.

Pressing & Stamping

The simplest, most spontaneous way to mark the clay surface is using your finger. Pressing into clay is a natural human response to a tactile material—children will do it automatically! Intentional dimple and nail marks were used as decoration on Stone and Bronze Age vessels. But aside from your fingers, there are a host of other marks to choose from and a variety of ways in which they can be used.

Impressions can be pressed more easily into soft clay, and will have a slightly different quality than those pressed into firm clay. With the latter, it's easier to make a crisp, shallow mark,

so consider which clay is more suitable for your piece before you begin. The intention with a pressed or stamped detail is to create depth that traps a shadow and allows the imprint to stand out—the deeper the imprint the bolder the shadow. All sorts of objects both made and found can be utilized as possible mark-making tools. Often it's the mundane object that yields a spectacular imprint. Utilizing the "ends of things" is a good starting point. You can try kitchen utensils, paintbrushes, sticks, dowels, the heads of screws, and the ends of keys, as well as natural items such as shells, rocks, and pieces of bark. Even soles of shoes can be good. Look around, investigate, and make some experimental imprints. With some consideration, the simplest stamp can be transformed into a sophisticated pattern or texture. Bear in mind that pressing some objects across a curved, three-dimensional surface can be difficult and may not yield the same result as a test done on a flat slab.

Glazing can further accentuate the surface, but make sure that the glaze isn't too thick, or it may smother the detail like a heavy blanket. Oxide washes and colored clay inlay can also enhance pattern and texture. Whether pressing into soft or hard clay, always be aware of the force that you're exerting and support the inside wall with your fingers or a tool.

Get to know what a tool can do and exploit its mark-making potential. Don't overlook common objects, which can be pressed repeatedly to make patterns. See the patterns on the facing page for examples.

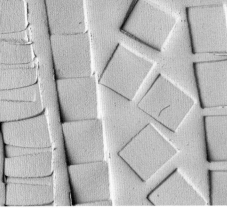

End of a **SQUARE DOWEL**

End of a **POTTER'S KNIFE HANDLE**

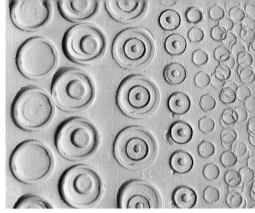

Back end of various **MARKER PENS**

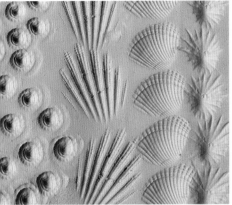

SHELLS

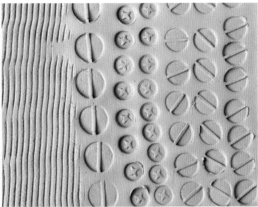

SCREWS

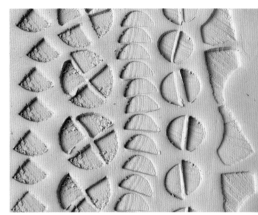

Ends of **VARIOUS TRIMS**

End of my **THUMB** pressed
quickly and deeply into soft clay

Tip of my **LITTLE FINGER** pressed lightly
into soft clay

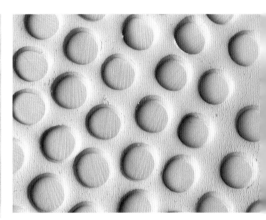

End of a **DOWEL** pressed deeply
into thick, soft clay

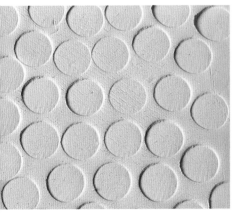

End of a **DOWEL** pressed
lightly into soft clay

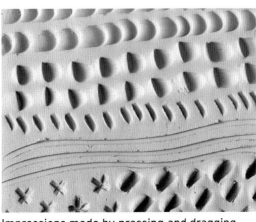

Impressions made by pressing and dragging
an **ICE-CREAM STICK** into soft clay

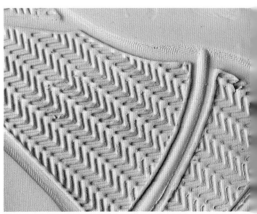

SOLE OF A SHOE pressed into
soft clay

Carving Clay

As with stamping and pressing, carving will yield different results depending on the consistency and texture of your clay. Smooth, hard clay will give a precise line, and soft, groggy clay will yield a more textural, vigorous mark; each has its own particular virtues to exploit. Any design, especially intricate ones, should be worked out on paper first. It's then transferred onto the pot by carefully retracing over the drawn lines with a sharp pencil, leaving a mark in the clay.

The secret of good carving is to remove clay, not just push it aside. It's a lot like making a linocut but here it is the clay that is gouged out. Carving with a needle or pencil will make a scruffy, torn line because the clay is forced apart as the tool plows through. Regardless of whether you want a subtle or bold cut, using the appropriate tool will allow you to peel away the clay, leaving a clean line. The tools I recommend are special loop tools available from pottery shops. They come in a range of shapes and sizes. Make sure to select ones that have metal loops that have been sharpened; they bite into the clay nicely. You can carve on smooth, hard clay with a knife tip or a stick with a chisel-shaped end, but I prefer the loop tools for the clean, accurate cuts they make. In summary, the state and texture of the clay and the tool employed will all have a bearing on the end result.

Shallow, incised lines are called sgraffito. Sgraffito can be carried out at any stage during the pot's drying. Sgraffito is often used as an effective technique for drawing through colored slips—an approach that we'll study later in the Slip chapter.

Glaze can be used to either heighten or soften the effect of incised surfaces. The results depend on the type and thickness of the glaze. All incised designs can be filled with colored clay or slip—this is called inlay and is similar to marquetry in woodwork. A contrasting color of clay, a little softer than the clay that is incised, is pushed firmly into the incisions so that it reaches all the nooks and crannies of the design. The inlay is not smoothed out but left proud on the surface to dry until it's leather hard. The whole surface is then scraped level using a tool such as the flat side of a steel rib. If the colored clay smears, let the piece dry further before scraping again.

For fine, shallow incisions such as sgraffito, I suggest using colored slip as the inlay. The slip must be yogurt thick and the surrounding clay leather hard. Flood the design with the slip. As it sinks in and firms up, you'll need to blob on another layer, and possibly a third. Don't worry that the slip goes far beyond the design; it all gets tidied up later [A]!

Leave the piece to get very firm, then start scraping with a metal rib [B]. If the colored clay begins to smear and stain around the design, let it dry further, then try again. It's perfectly possible to have a neat, crisp design.

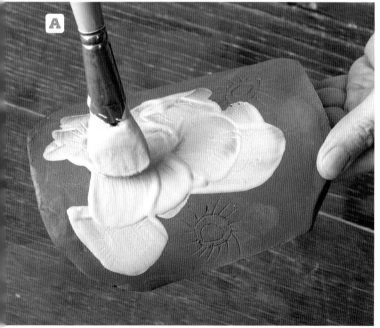

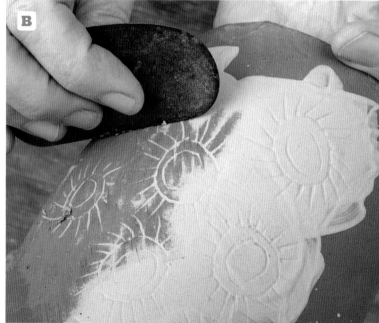

CARVING DEEPLY These design elements were made using various loop tools and chisel-ended sticks to carve deeply into soft clay. A bold effect was accomplished by carving deeply through groggy, leather-hard clay.

SGRAFFITO These shallow marks and patterns were made using a chisel-ended stick drawn through a layer of leather-hard slip.

SHALLOW CARVINGS The carving technique used for pictorial effect. Using the loop and chisel-ended tools, more clay is removed, leaving a raised image.

SGRAFFITO SLIP has been inlaid into shallow incisions.

INLAID Deeply gouged incisions are being inlaid with colored clay.

Relief Surfaces

This is clay applied to the surface of the vessel to give a raised design; it ranges from very low to very high. To get the most control, attach the relief when the pot is leather hard. Make sure everything you join on is slipped first. Consider the practical needs of your pot and choose the appropriate kind of relief. An object that requires much daily handling would not be a good candidate for really high course relief, but a flowerpot would! The higher the relief, the more sculptural the effect. Don't feel that you have to wallpaper the entire vessel; relief can be just as effective when used selectively.

CUT AND APPLIED RELIEF

From a thinly rolled slab of clay, you can cut shapes and add them directly to the surface of the pot—rather like you would when decorating a pie with pastry leaves.

Lightly sketch out the shapes on the soft slab and sketch their placement onto the pot with a pencil. Draw faintly, as you may want to reposition pieces as the design develops. Cut out the shapes with a sharp knife, making sure not to let them dry out, and attach them to the pot with slip. Press the pieces firmly in place with a wide flat stick or batten; this is much neater and more affective than fingertips, and there's the added advantage that the shapes will soften and spread under the pressure of the stick, making them less harsh [C]. You can work back into the relief with sticks to create more delicate details.

Since it's the shadow that shows the depth, the clay shapes can be just a few millimeters thick and still create enough definition to be effective. However, I encourage you to chunky them up if you want a more sculptural, tactile surface. This kind of relief is even more wonderful when glazed!

COILS AS RELIEF

Soft snakes of clay (any thickness or length) can be used on the surface to give another form of textural relief. Press them into position using slip, wiping a fingertip down each side to help join and disguise the seam. Then squeeze or pinch the snakes to make them thinner or taller, or let each pinch mark show to create a scalloped effect. Rather than pinching and extending, try tooling along the top of each coil with a series of repeated marks, or dimple using your fingertips. Coils can be applied to create linear or swirl effects [D].

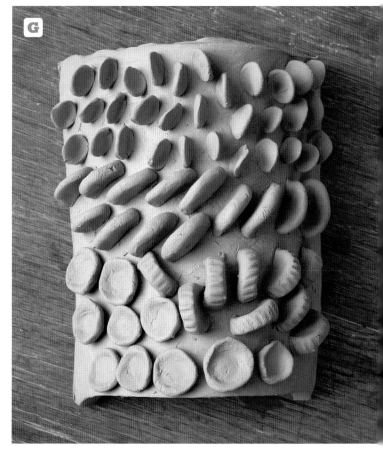

BUMPY RELIEF

A surface of repeated bumps made from soft balls of clay can be a tactile and effective surface treatment. Roll a soft ball of clay between your fingers, dab slip onto the pot, press it on firmly without over flattening, and form and shape it further to make it rounded or pointy. You can alter the surface of the bumps and adjust their size by pressing in all kinds of tools. Try perforating the bumps with holes or making a single cratered center. Slicing off the tops is another option, as is pressing each bump flat as you join it on to give the bumps a scale-like quality [E]. Simple alterations can be very effective. A bead of soft clay pressed onto the pot and thumbed away on one side becomes a petal-like shape—a striking yet unobtrusive surface treatment [F].

PINCHED DISK RELIEF

Soft balls of clay of different sizes can be pinched and flattened between your fingers into disks of varying thicknesses. When cut into halves and applied to the surface, a scaly, hedgehog-like texture emerges that can look very animated. The edges of the disks can be made more decorative with the addition of a pattern or texture; try rolling the disks like wheels over corrugated cardboard or other coarse textures. Pinching the clay when it's drier will cause cracking around the edges, which, if controlled and repeated, could be very effective. Cut and join the relief shapes when they are leather hard so as not to spoil the detail [G].

JULIE WHITMORE Julie has been a potter since 1996. She studied art at Fullerton College in Fullerton, California, and is a graduate of Santa Barbara College. She has exhibited her work in numerous shows, including the Twining Teapot Show at the York Art Gallery in York, England, and Art in Bloom at the Santa Barbara Museum of Art. Julie lives in Cambria, California. She blogs at juliewhitmorepottery.blogspot.com.

A *DONKEY AND HOLLYHOCKS*, 2012, 5″ (12.7 cm) wide x 3″ (7.6 cm) high **B** *RABBIT CUP*, 2012, 3″ (7.6 cm) wide x 2¹/₂″ (6.4 cm) high **C** *CHICKEN IN THE FLOWERBED*, 2012, 3¹/₂″ (8.9 cm) wide x 3″ (7.6 cm) high **D** *LEAPING RAM*, 2012, 6″ (15.2 cm) wide x 3″ (7.6 cm) high **E** *SHEEP UNDER PLUM TREE*, 2012, 6¹/₂″ (16.5 cm) wide x 3″ (7.6 cm) high

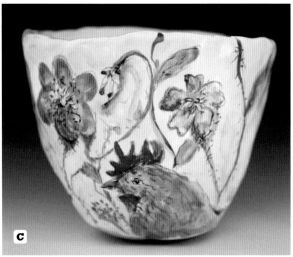

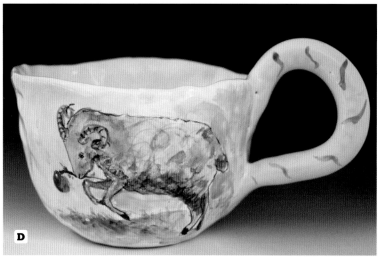

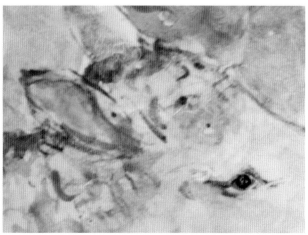

VICKI GRIMA As editor of *The Journal of Australian Ceramics* and executive officer of the Australian Ceramics Association, Vicki is in daily contact with the national and international ceramics communities. She squeezes her ceramics practice in alongside the work she does in these key positions. Nature, with its irregular repetitions, delicate intricacies, and inherent patterns, serves as a major inspiration for her work. Vicki has taught and exhibited throughout Australia. To learn more about her work, visit www.vickigrima.com.au.

F *87 SPOONS PROJECT, THREE TWO-PIECE SETS*, 2011, Each approx $^3/_4$'' (2 cm) high x 3$^1/_8$'' (8 cm) wide x 2$^3/_8$'' (6 cm) deep porcelain and raku clay **G** *87 SPOONS PROJECT*, 2011, each 2 to 4$^3/_8$'' (5 to 11 cm) in length, porcelain **H** *87 SPOONS PROJECT, 3-PIECE SET*, 2011, $^3/_4$'' (2 cm) high x 4$^3/_4$'' (12 cm) wide x 2$^{15}/_{16}$'' (7.5 cm) deep, porcelain and raku clay **I** *GROUP OF THREE PORCELAIN PINCH POTS*, 2008, Each 2$^3/_8$'' to 3$^1/_8$'' (6 to 8 cm) high x 2$^3/_8$'' to 3$^1/_8$'' (6 to 8 cm) wide approx, porcelain

COLOR & GLAZE

One of the unique advantages to working in clay is the kaleidoscope of glazes and ceramic colors at the potter's disposal. The number of choices can be dizzying but hosts tremendous potential, allowing for a vast range of exciting interpretation. This chapter details the main types of glazes and ceramic colorants in order to help clarify what is best for your work.

INTRODUCING COLOR

There are several materials, in both powder and liquid form, that can be used to create colorful decoration directly on the unfired or bisque-fired clay surface. Each has its own distinctive characteristics and color range that can vary drastically depending on the type of glaze it's with, firing temperature, and kiln atmosphere.

Slips

Using slips is a versatile and easy way of getting color and pattern onto the unfired pot. Made from a mixture of clay and water and mixed to a smooth, creamy consistency, slips are simple, inexpensive to prepare, and can be applied using a wide variety of techniques.

The simplest slip can be made by mixing some dry clay with water. Of course, it won't show up unless it's a contrasting color. Slip can be thinned down to make it more translucent or made thicker for a more opaque look. The two weights can be combined to lend variation and depth to your decoration.

After bisque firing, slips look dry and the color is subdued. To enrich and bring out the true color of the slip, apply a clear or lightly tinted glaze and re-fire the piece. However, on pieces that don't need to be watertight, such as flowerpots, slips with strong color contrasts—black and white, for example—can be fired without the need of a shiny glaze. The resulting surfaces will be drier and more muted, but perfectly sufficient for decorative purposes. Preparation methods and slip recipes are in the back of the book. You can also buy pre-prepared slips from some ceramic suppliers.

The optimum time to apply a decorating slip is when the clay is firm but not quite leather hard. To do so when the pot is still too soft can result in the clay splitting and collapsing as it becomes oversaturated with the water in the slip. Apply it too late and it fails to bond with the surface of the clay, flaking off in the bisque or glaze firing.

Oxides and stains are powdered pigments used to color both glazes and slips. Oxides are generally the more powerful colorant but stains have a broader palette. They are compatible and together can create interesting color effects.

OXIDES

These are naturally occurring metallic minerals that are sold as powders. They're used to color glazes, slips, and clay, but can also be used neat (mixed with water) to make a direct painting solution on top of an unfired glaze. Technically, this is called inglaze painting, as the oxides sink into the unfired glaze, then fuse together in the glaze firing. As well as being brushed, oxides can be sponged, splashed, or flicked onto the surface.

Oxide colors—like blues, greens, blacks, purples, grays, and browns—are earthy and natural. This may sound unappealing, but there's a richness and depth to oxide colors that the commercial equivalents (stains) don't have. In their raw state, most of them are nothing like their eventual fired color.

Oxides are made of heavy particles that tend to settle quickly when held in a watery solution; this can make application difficult. To help keep them in suspension, try mixing them with milk instead of water. This painterly mix should be about the consistency of watercolor paint. However, oxides vary in potency, and some may require more or less dilution. The strongest oxide colors are cobalt and copper. They can be bought in both oxide or carbonate form. Carbonates are less concentrated, but are still powerful colorants. A white glaze with the addition of 0.5% cobalt carbonate will make a rich blue glaze, whereas the same glaze with the addition of 0.5% red iron oxide will barely be altered. As with many aspects of glazes, trial and error through simple testing will always be beneficial.

As I've said, glaze type and kiln temperature are huge factors in the outcome of the final appearance of oxide decoration. At lower temperatures (earthenware) and in conjunction with white glazes, the colors will always be brighter and more intense. This painted ware is often called Majolica, and is, historically, an ancient form of ceramic decoration. Majolica is worth looking at for inspiration for surface design and decoration. The same principle can be carried out on white stoneware glazes, though the colors will be speckled and even more natural looking because they react to a greater degree with the glaze and kiln atmosphere. In the reduction firing, oxide colors can alter enormously depending on the ingredients in the glaze beneath and the absence of oxygen in the kiln atmosphere: copper oxide can be red, and red iron oxide can be green. Others oxides, such as vanadium and rutile, can also become quite reactive.

STAINS

The main difference between these materials and oxides are the colors. The range is extensive, offering a true rainbow palette of reds, oranges, pinks, yellows, blues, purples, and more. The fired colors can have a paint-like appearance in that they're somewhat flat, unlike oxides, which have natural variation. The predictable nature of stains is perhaps part of their attraction, as there's no element of risk, like with oxides.

Usually purchased as a powder, they mix easily with water. To use a stain as a decorating medium under or over unfired glazes, I suggest mixing it with the glaze that you're using on the pot—preferably a clear or white glaze that won't affect the color of the stain. This mixture will help it to adhere. The glaze will bind with the stain, making it more stable during use and less likely to smudge. Stains can be applied, like oxides, by brushing, sponging, and so on. They can be diluted to create areas of color wash or kept thicker and therefore more opaque, for smaller areas of decoration. Some stain colors are unstable at high temperatures, resulting in loss of color. Always check the labeling for the maximum firing temperature. Powdered stains can be combined with oxides to extend and enliven the color possibilities. As with all ceramic experiments, careful documentation and testing should be carried out first to avoid disappointment.

Glazes

Glazes are thin, liquid coatings of glass, applied to the surface of a bisque-fired pot, that melt and fuse when heated in a kiln. The result is a hard, watertight coating. Within this simple procedure is infinite scope for color and texture, opening up a whole field of surface exploration. I want to warn you that any glazed parts of a pot that are in contact with the kiln shelf will become glued to it during firing so glaze should always be wiped from the foot of a pot before firing. Give more clearance on the lower outside edges for those glassy glazes that are known to be runnier.

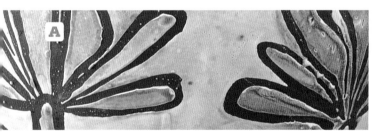

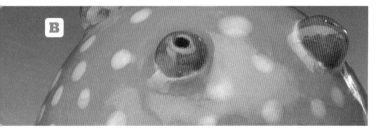

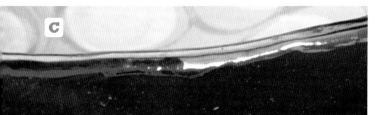

With the application of a glaze, you're presented with many exciting choices regarding the final appearance of your pot. Glazes can be clear, shiny, matt, scaly, satin, and all things in between. With glazing, there arises the opportunity to decorate and pattern the surface, which lends another level of interest. Remember that color is another language—a black matt glaze will communicate in a different way than a shiny pink one. Some surfaces repel and others invite, so consider these qualities when dressing your pot.

Keep in mind that the color of your glaze can be dramatically different depending on the color of your clay. White clays will always give a brighter result, just as if you were painting on white paper versus brown paper. However, some glazes perform better on clays that have iron in them (the tan and brown bodies), making them warmer and less harsh. It's worth testing a sample of glaze first. Make small tiles of differing clays, about the size of a playing card. After bisque firing, apply three distinct, overlapping zones of a single glaze and then re-fire. Notice how different clays affect the outcome, and how even within one glaze there can be interest and variation according to thickness. Be sure to keep a record of your tests for later reference. After glazing, but before firing, write the glaze name and any other important details on the back of the tile using a mix of red iron oxide and water.

PREPARED ONGLAZE COLORS

Ready-mixed, liquid onglaze colors are an exciting way to explore surface decoration [A]. Onglaze, as the term suggests, means applied to the surface of the glaze, before firing. Subsequently, the glaze and the onglaze fuse together. Naturally, the two elements must be compatible according to temperature. They're typically low fire. Onglaze colors are most often used in conjunction with white or transparent glazes, which allows the colors on top to stay vibrant. Compatible, ready-mixed glazes are usually sold by the onglaze's manufacturer, but you can make your own; you'll find some recipes in the back of this book. Onglaze colors are consistent and reliable, which makes them fun and easy to use. These painterly pots of glaze are available in a wide range of natural and vibrant colors. Use them directly from the bottle and apply them with any kind of brush or sponge. Dilute them with water, and you can wash them over large areas as a background color or build them up in translucent layers, which will give your decoration more depth. Try using them in conjunction with latex or emulsion wax, masking off large areas of color while you build up additional layers of new color. Or, apply the wax decoration first, before washing, over the diluted onglaze, rather as you would if doing a crayon and wash painting. All the colors are compatible, so you can overlap and intermix colors to extend range. As with stains and underglazes, the predictable nature of manufactured color can look flat and paint-like. Consider softening the appearance by decorating a piece with both underglazes and oxides. Again, some experimentation can help avoid mishaps and allow for repeated success.

UNDERGLAZES

Not surprisingly, underglazes [B] are the opposite of onglazes. They are applied to the bisque-fired pot before glazing. Sold as small pots of thick liquid, they look and feel just like prepared onglazes, but come in an even wider color range. Also like onglazes, underglazes require a brush and/or sponge for application, but they are not suitable for thin washes, as the colors can look insubstantial, and some, especially reds, won't register at all unless applied thickly. Three coats is the standard application. Colors can usually be overlapped and usually intermixed. When fired without a glaze finish, they have a dry quality, not unlike fired slip. They're at their most vibrant when covered with transparent glaze because anything too opaque will mask the color. Compatible brush-on glazes are sold together with underglazes.

LUSTRES

These are very pure metallic oxides, sold as liquids and applied to a fired and glazed surface, then re-fired at a low temperature (optimum temp 1472°F [800°C]) in order to fuse. Although permanent, the finished lustre surface is relatively soft and can be abraded over time.

I'm recommending lustres not as an overall finish, but as something used to embellish and highlight [C]. There are several reasons for this. First is expense. Lustres are costly, especially gold and silver varieties. They're sold in tiny bottles and look like thin, black molasses. Secondly, a stylistic caution: use lustres judiciously, as they can look brash when blanketing an entire form. You will often see lustres applied in bands to decorate rims on teacups and plates; gold is commonly used for this finishing effect. They could be used effectively to delineate elements of surface decoration or to draw attention to a lip or handle of a form. The surface you apply a lustre to must be absolutely grease-free, otherwise the lustre will not stay smooth and even. Lustres must be completely dry before they can be fired.

As well as the opaque gold, silver, and bronze, iridescent lustres are also available. Being transparent, they're subtler, lending a veiled, pearlized quality. Lustres can be brushed or sponged onto any fired glaze surface, but will be more muted over darker glazes. During firing, they give off a resinous smell that is unpleasant. If you don't have a fan to vent your kiln, open windows and leave the room; the smell doesn't last long.

Making Versus Buying Glazes

Glazes can be mixed from scratch (from powdered chemical ingredients) or bought pre-prepared from ceramic suppliers. There are benefits to using glazes from both the handmade and purchased categories and one shouldn't exclude the other. The more choices you have, the more successful your finished pottery will be, and each option has its own benefits and drawbacks.

MAKING

THE PROS: 1) In the long run, you'll save money by mixing your own glazes. 2) One of the prime reasons for going the homemade route is the flexibility you'll have regarding choice. There are thousands of glaze recipes available in books and online, and with a little glaze knowledge, you'll be able to alter or recreate recipes to your exact preference. 3) Mixing your own glaze allows for a broader scope when it comes to methods of application such as dipping and pouring which are quick and economical ways to apply glazes, and allow for exciting overlapping of different colors.

THE CONS: 1) The initial investment to acquire the ingredients is likely to be significant. To mix glazes from scratch, you'll need to have available a variety of raw powdered materials, strong containers with well-fitting lids, and room enough to store them in. 2) Some of the materials are toxic (but with sensible handling and precautions they shouldn't pose a health risk). 3) There is also another investment required to make your own: time. As in cooking, measuring out ingredients, sieving them, testing them, and cleaning up can eat into precious working time.

When mixing your own glazes, a bit of glaze chemistry knowledge is desirable. Understanding the rudiments of glaze theory isn't as daunting as it first seems. Each ingredient in the glaze is performing a certain task. For example, one part is the glass element, one part is the stiffener (to stop the glass from running off the pot), another may be a matting agent, and another ingredient may lend color. It's really no more complex than a list of cake ingredients! I do advise that anyone wishing to get involved in glaze making take a class or two first. Many craft or art centers offer such workshops that are specially aimed at beginners. A little knowledge will go a long way.

BUYING

THE PROS: Pluses for buying pre-mixed glazes have to do, as with any pre-prepared product, with convenience. 1) They require less storage space. 2) The results are consistent and reliable, assuming you stick to application/firing guidelines. A broad, albeit somewhat limited range of colors and textures are available, including bright colors for higher firing temperatures. 3) Application is very straightforward—either by sponge or brush—and the drying time between layers (three layers is the usual recommendation) is very fast. 4) You don't need any glaze knowledge in order to use them; everything you need to know is printed on the label.

THE CONS: 1) Despite the wide selection of pre-mixed glazes, you may not find exactly what you're looking for, so some compromise may be necessary. 2) Most commercially prepared liquid glazes are applied by brushing, with three even coats being the standard to achieve the correct color/ texture. If you have several large pieces to glaze, this can be tedious and time consuming (as opposed to dipping and pouring). In order to dip a pot into a glaze you need a fairly large quantity—even for a mug you need enough to submerge it. Most purchased glazes come ready-mixed in quantities that are not sufficient to immerse a pot, so they prepare the glaze in a special way so that it can be applied evenly with a brush. Sometimes you can buy a ready-mixed glaze in a gallon container, but the range is more limited and very expensive.

A Safety Note on Glazes and Glaze Materials

Care must always be taken when mixing and handling glazes and glaze ingredients. When weighing powdered materials, avoid making dust, as some chemicals are toxic. Always wear a mask and rubber gloves when weighing and mxing glazes. Do not eat or drink while preparing and using them. Wipe up spills immediately, and wear an apron or protective clothing that can be washed after use. Store all raw materials and glazes in unbreakable airtight containers, and clearly label them.

DECORATING & GLAZING TECHNIQUES

Glazes and slips share similar application techniques, the only difference being the state of the clay beneath—slips go on raw clay, glazes on bisque-fired clay. Some shapes lend themselves more to certain techniques than others and the quantity of slip or glaze may also dictate your choice of application. It's standard practice to apply glaze or slip to the inside of a pot before proceeding to the outside. The following application methods are simple, but only with repetition will you become skilled.

Brushing

I recommend using brushes made from natural hair as opposed to synthetic. These brushes will hold more liquid and give you a livelier, more responsive mark. Use small, fine brushes for detail work and large, floppy brushes for expressive, dramatic strokes of color and splashy patterns. You may want to apply one solid area of color that shows the texture of the brush strokes; your options are as varied as if you were using paint. A solid, light background will be a good foundation for brighter colors. Try to make your brush strokes swift and definite—ideally in one or two movements—before loading up the brush with more slip or glaze and repeating across the pot surface [D]. If layering different colors in a painterly fashion, let the liquid beneath become touch dry, or dry enough to touch without coming off on your fingers, before working on top so as not to disturb and muddy the individual colors.

I must stress that over-brushing slip (spreading it back and forth as you might do when painting a wall) can cause color contamination, as the clay beneath will begin to blend into the mix.

Sponging

This technique can be used to create a printed texture or individual, decorative motifs. It's most effective when applied to a smooth surface.

You can use natural or synthetic sponges for overall coverage. Do be aware that for a more even finish, you'll get the best results from a sponge that has a fine texture. Large-holed sponges are better for creating deliberate textures. Cut the sponge to a manageable size. Fill a saucer with slip or glaze that has the consistency of thick yogurt (if using oxide or stain they should be more thin, like milk). Dip the sponge in, wipe off the excess liquid on the rim of the saucer, and press the sponge up and down in one movement onto the pot. You may get two or three prints from the sponge before you have to replenish it. Overlap the print just a little so as not to leave gaps, and change the angle of the sponge to avoid making a repeat pattern, unless that's your desired effect [E]. You can change colors as you go, or apply a second and third layer to create a more veiled appearance. Make sure the underlying layer is dry to the touch before you add the next layer.

To create patterns, use a synthetic sponge, as it'll have a finer grain. Cut it into simple geometric shapes like circles, squares, and triangles, dip it into the slip or glaze, and press and stamp as described above.

Splashing & Flicking

This decorating method creates a speckled, almost marble-like pattern on a piece—think Jackson Pollock on pottery [F]. Several layers of different colors can be used, and, with care, the clay beneath completely concealed. Each layer of slip or glaze must be touch dry before you proceed with the next, otherwise the combination may start to run.

There are two methods of application. The first is to dip your fingertips into slip or glaze that's the consistency of yogurt, hold them a few inches away from the pot, and literally flick your fingers at the pot. You may have to replenish with slip after a couple of flicks. The type of splash mark that you get will vary depending on the distance between your fingers and the pot. The closer they are, the bigger the marks will be. A longer splash mark will result if your fingers are held at a more acute angle.

Turning the form and changing the direction of the flick will help create even coverage. The same action repeated over and over will tend to give a directional rhythm to the marks that you may or may not want.

Brushes can also be utilized to give a similar effect. Those that have stiff bristles—toothbrushes, scrubbing brushes, and the like—are most effective. If you have a large pot, consider using a broom head (one with natural bristles) for a quick and vigorous attack! The principle is the same as above, distance and angle continuing to have a bearing on the effect of the marks, but here the size and number of bristles is a factor to consider. A toothbrush will give a spray of fine speckles; a broom head will give a magnified version of the same marks. Whatever brush you use, dip it in the slip or

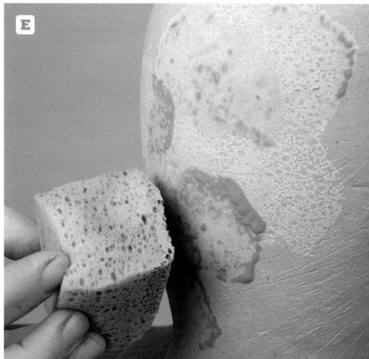

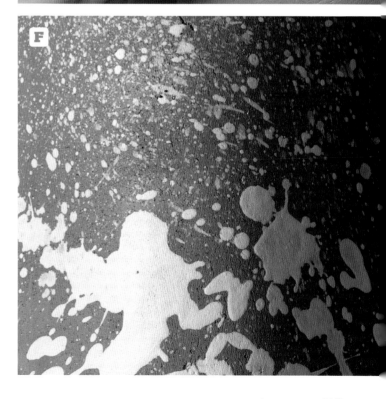

glaze, gently tap off the excess, hold it bristle-side up, and run your thumb, fingertip, or side of your hand across the top from front to back. You can move it around the pot to distribute the speckles more evenly.

Before launching onto a finished piece I recommend practicing both methods first. A good fake pot could be a sheet of stiff paper rolled into a wide tube. Both approaches could be very effective if used in conjunction with a paper stencil or latex wax, allowing for specific control of splashed patterned areas (i.e. stripes of splashed texture). Both oxides and stains mixed with water can be applied as described above.

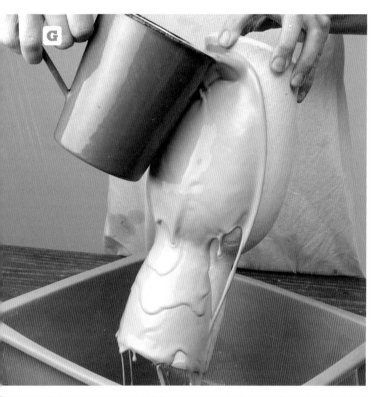

Pouring & Dipping

If you want a really smooth, dense covering of slip/glaze, dipping and pouring are the best techniques to use. The consistency should be a little more fluid than for brushing and trailing. In both instances, you need to hold the pot in one hand with widely spread fingertips that make firm but minimal contact while the slip/glaze is being applied. Some pot shapes will lend themselves better to pouring and dipping than others. Forms with very round bases and no feet may be impractical to dip; consider brushing or sponging the liquid on to such pieces. In both instances, whether dipping or pouring, parts of the pot that were in contact with your fingertips will remain uncovered. When the piece has been righted, you can easily correct these bald areas with a quick touch-up.

To pour slip or glaze, hold the pot upside down over a bucket, and, with a full jug of liquid, quickly pour it around the outside in a continuous veil, turning the vessel with your hand as you go **[G]**. Give the pot a firm downward shake to release any excess. Carefully turn it over and slide it onto a board. Try not to touch the freshly coated surface.

To dip, fill a container that's deeper and wider than the pot containing the slip/glaze. Take into account the fact that at least one of your hands has to fit into the container when holding the piece. Make sure you have a firm grip on the pot—try putting your thumb on the base and your index and middle fingers on the rim. Dip the pot straight down into the liquid. For glaze, keep it submerged for about three seconds, but only a quick dip in and out for slip—no lingering **[H]**! As with pouring, give the pot a swift jerk and shake to release any excess. Carefully maneuver the piece right-side up and onto a board, and then quickly drop a spot or two of slip or glaze onto any finger marks.

In both cases, you have the option to dip or pour onto specific areas, creating zones or bands of contrasting color. The shape of the poured or dipped liquid may remind you of something else—perhaps you see a tree, a fish, or a head. Consider developing the image further by using sgraffito or brushwork; a simple pattern could fill the shape. It's really worth looking at Japanese Oribe pottery to see some marvelous interpretations of this theme.

Wiping Through

Slip or glaze that has been dipped or poured and is still wet and fluid can be wiped or combed through to create soft fluid marks that have a pleasing raised quality—think of the pattern in wet sand just after a wave has retreated. To be most effective, there should be a strong contrast of color between the slip or glaze and the pot. For instance, white slip poured over red earthenware clay and then wiped through will reveal dark lines. The combing can literally be carried out with a wide-toothed comb, forks, or at least two fingers [I]. Whatever tool you use, the movement must be spontaneous and sweeping. Keep patterns simple; lines, swirls, waves, and thumb dots will all be very effective.

Sgraffito

This is a wonderful technique with a long history as a means of ceramic decoration. While sgraffito can be carried out using glaze on a bisque-fired pot, it is normally performed with slip on pre-fired clay. A thin layer of differently colored slip is brushed, dipped, or poured onto the pot and left to become leather hard. A design is then scratched through the slip to reveal the clay beneath [J]. The type of carved line will depend on the tool you use; a wide array of effects can be achieved. In most cases, I think the best results are to be had with a wooden tool that has a chisel-like end, since this allows the clay to be removed neatly with a clean edge. Try not to gouge into the clay beneath, but simply peel away the coating of slip. You can try using the ends of paintbrushes and wooden ice cream sticks—even coffee stirrers. As with all decorating approaches, but especially with sgraffito, I advise you to plan your design in advance. Use a pencil to lightly sketch out the design directly onto the leather-hard slip; this will cut down on the chance for error.

Slip Trailing

This is a bit like icing a cake. Thick, smooth slip or glaze is squeezed out of a slip trailer, which is a rubber bulb fitted with a fine nozzle [K]. These can be purchased at a pottery supplier, though I've also seen them in the baby aisle at the pharmacy. If you choose, you may improvise and use a small plastic bottle like one you might find at the drugstore for applying hair dye, but I personally think the rubber versions are easier and more pleasant to use.

It's certainly easier to slip trail liquid on a more horizontal surface, but simple designs such as dots, stripes, and wavy lines can be carried out successfully on a vertical plane. Slip trailing has a marvelous history dating back hundreds of years. European slipware of the 17th and 18th centuries is a particularly exciting period of production and is certainly worth looking at for inspiration.

I strongly recommend that before applying slip or glaze to a piece, you practice drawing with slip/glaze on a piece of paper so that you get the feel of the tool and the amount of pressure needed to get a good line. Your movements and hand rhythm should be quite fast, just as if you were writing.

Make sure to fill the slip trailer as full as possible and shake the liquid down into the nozzle so as not to trap any air. To get the slip or glaze into the bulb or bottle, squeeze it firmly before dipping the nozzle into the liquid. Release the pressure and the liquid should get sucked in. If that doesn't happen, your mixture may be too thick. It should be stiff enough that the drawn lines are raised without any bleeding or blurring.

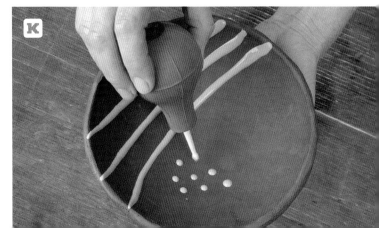

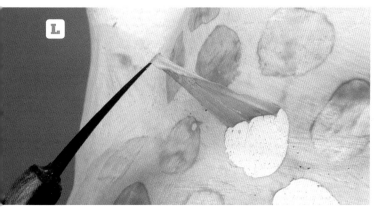

Stenciling

Using stencils is a simple, effective way of creating contrasting areas of color based on a positive/negative masking. The stencil is applied to leather-hard clay or bisque ware and then covered with slip or glaze. Before the slip/glaze dries completely, ideally when it's touch dry, the stencil is removed, revealing the color of the clay or glaze beneath [L]. Within this approach are many possibilities for interpretation, from bold and abstract to delicate and detailed. Much will depend on the type of stencil you use. For example, torn paper shapes are excellent for simple punchy designs [M], whereas wax resist stencils will allow for finer graphic work. Leaves and flowers can also be used effectively. You can mix and combine stencil techniques to build up complex layers of colors and marks, resulting in an interesting surface that has lots of visual depth. There's also the option to combine it with other techniques such as sponge and brush; it really is very versatile, lending itself to a collage-like approach. Most stencils are removed before firing, but there are some, such as wax emulsion, that stay on until they are burnt off in the heat of the kiln.

SLIP GALLERY Here are six samples showing some typical decorative approaches to using slip. These techniques can also be carried out with glazes for a similar effect with one exception, sgraffito, which, due to the nature of damp glaze, will have a slightly scratchier appearance.

BRUSHED

SPONGED

WIPED

SGRAFFITO

SLIP TRAILED

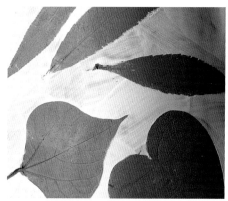

STENCILED

THE DECORATED SURFACE

Decorating a pot is rather like dressing it up. We know that certain patterns and colors can be worn more successfully by some people than others. It's the same with pots. Before leaping in with glaze and brush, you must consider the shape of the piece and what is going to enhance the form rather than detract. Through its proportions, your pot will have a personality that must be taken into account.

A plain form with no handles or lids competing for attention is essentially a three-dimensional canvas, and offers more scope for surface treatment. A complex sculptural form with spout, lid, knob, or handle elements, needs greater consideration. Balancing a decorative design necessitates sketching and planning in order to achieve harmony between surface and form.

PATTERNS

The word "pattern" can be misleading because it conjures up an image of a tightly repeated design. And yes, this is one way of looking at it, but it can be represented more broadly. First, bear in mind the issue of symmetry versus asymmetry, and within this, the possibilities of naturalistic, stylized, geometric, abstract, and even text-based designs. Decoration can also be more literal, as in the pictorial tradition of landscapes, figures, etcetera. Another painterly interpretation could be a single motif, like a cameo-style portrait. The spectrum has no boundaries.

You'll notice that many designs and patterns appearing on ceramics, whether historical or contemporary, are ubiquitous; altered occasionally but essentially the same, they appear across time and within various civilizations, and are still in use by potters and designers today. Many of these patterns are simple, stylized repetitions—cross-hatched lines, bands, rhythmic spots and circles, swirls and serifs—that continue to be a valid means of decoration and not to be overlooked.

Sources

There are many fertile hunting grounds for finding patterns, gathering ideas, and wallowing in inspiration. In your journey for research, always make a record of your finds, drawing and photographing examples as you go for adaptation in the studio later.

↠ **Early ceramics.** The first designs on pottery were bold, simple, and quite abstract, becoming more naturalized as early man looked to the natural world as a source from which to derive ideas.

↠ **Nature.** Flora and fauna continue to be rich areas of discovery for designers and can perhaps be starting points for your own adventures in pattern making. You can use nature literally, as with using leaves as stencils.

↠ **Textiles.** This is another area rich with design. All kinds of carpets, rugs, clothes, and fabrics offer a vast array of source material.

↠ **Paper.** Within the paper world too, patterns abound. Wallpaper, wrapping paper, paper bags, and confectionary wrappers—especially the foil variety—are worthwhile areas of investigation.

↠ **Other craft disciplines.** These too can yield interesting results. Metalwork on all scales (from jewelry to railings), stained glass windows, lacework, mosaic floors and walls, trellises, and grilles all can harbor useable patterns.

And of course looking at ceramics should be an early port of call. Whether historical or contemporary, in a museum, a book, or your kitchen cupboard at home—a wealth of information is waiting to inspire and excite you.

Adapting a Design

This research is all very well, but what to do with it next? Copying directly and hoping that it will work on your pot is inadvisable. You must learn how to extract information and adapt it for the materials and form at hand.

Practice Builds Confidence and a Steady Hand

Marking a blank surface, while sometimes an irresistible temptation, can also be terrifying! Anyone who has ever wielded an icing bag over a birthday cake knows the shaky hand syndrome and the resulting wobbly decoration. The only way to overcome this nervousness is practice. As with all things clay, repetition pays off.

Painting on the vertical or on a curved form is a very different experience than working flat, and if you're going to be working directly with brushes and slips, glazes, or oxides, the following exercise is worth practicing to warm you up for the real thing. Once you've sketched and planned out your design on paper, transfer it onto a plain paper cup or bowl. Then paint 10 cups with the same design. With each attempt you should feel more relaxed; the marks you make will become a little more spontaneous and start to have a character that is personal to you—rather like a signature.

WORKING FROM TISSUE PAPER

In this exercise I began with the sheet of black and white tissue paper shown above as my starting point. Using a brush and ink and inspired by the graphic designs of the paper, I let my imagination run and doodled the motifs you see below. Notice how I isolated individual elements and then played with scale and spacing. Minimizing and maximizing and then regrouping the motifs allowed me to explore many creative possibilities and to extract several effective designs from one source. Working from positive to negative is also a quick way to change the feel of your design.

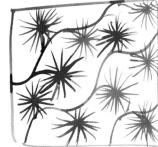

WORKING FROM PRINTED FABRIC

I followed a similar creative exercise as with the tissue paper except using the scrap of material pictured above. The fabric features quite a complicated design, so to copy it directly onto a pot would be an arduous and misleading task. By editing the information, by which I mean isolating some of the repeated elements, changing the color, and stylizing the floral motifs, I've created a new design that's more appropriate for a ceramic surface [A]. As you can see in [B], the pattern can be altered a step further by concentrating the spacing. Notice that in both instances, I'm not drawing with a pencil. By using a more fluid, tactile medium such as paint, ink, and pastel, you get closer to creating a design that is more akin to working with glazes and slips.

Figures C and D feature two basic patterns created using torn tissue paper. Both could be translated using ceramic techniques without sacrificing too much of the original design's quality. The stripes could be recreated with contrasting glazes, oxide washes, or underglazes, allowing for the third color bar as the stripes overlap [C]. The big blousy flowers might be recreated as a torn paper stencil (positive or negative) with painted slips, or as a sponge print [D].

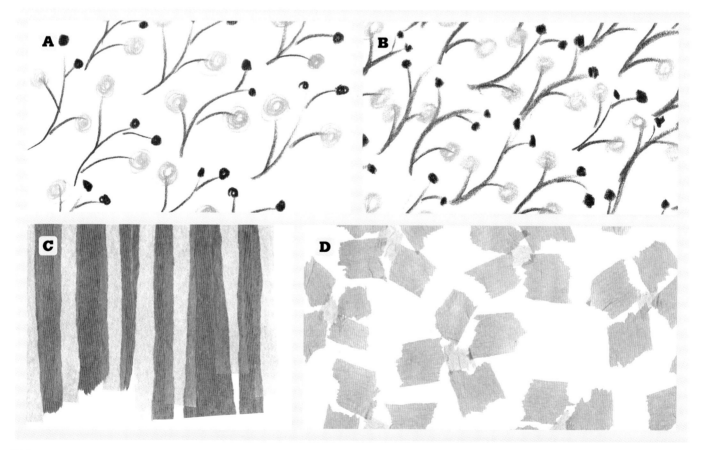

Don't be misled into thinking that complex, intricate patterns are more virtuous than simple ones. A little goes a long way. Any mark repeated will evolve into a pattern—a fingerprint scattered across the pot surface will make a pleasing array of dots. I want to reassure you that simple can be sophisticated and effective. The dot, line, and circle are worthy elements for masses of good pattern making and are essentially all you need for hundreds of good ideas. In the gallery of doodles below, I'm demonstrating the versatility of common, everyday marks, and how, when such marks are used in various combinations, the pattern making options are greatly increased. The first group (below) shows some ways of developing circle-based designs. Evolution of straight line designs can be seen in the second doodle group (page 62). Other variations include square designs, dot and ball combinations, and simple, floral motifs (all on page 63). The intention was to exhaust creative possibilities by making small changes, either by regrouping and resizing the marks, shifting the layout (placement could be symmetrical [linear, grid format] asymmetrical [random]), or altering the rhythm. These techniques can lend more movement, while juxtaposing different scales brings another exciting dimension. Of course, these are monotone patterns—imagine how exciting it is when you introduce color!

CIRCLE-BASED DESIGNS

HOOPS (THIN BRUSH)

HOOPS (FAT BRUSH)

POSITIVE/NEGATIVE

CONCENTRIC

CIRCLES WITHIN CIRCLES

SPIRALS

INFILL

BACKFILL

SCALLOPED

NUCLEUS

LINES WITHIN

LINES OUT

STRAIGHT-LINE DESIGNS

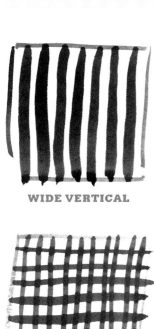

WIDE VERTICAL

CHANGE BRUSHSTROKE

HORIZONTAL

DIAGONAL

PLAID

DIAGONAL CRISSCROSS

COMBINING THICKNESS

GROUPING

LADDER LINES

HERRINGBONE

ZIGZAG

BASKETLIKE DASHES

CROSS VARIATIONS

DIAMOND LINES

LINEAR COMBINATIONS

SQUARE DESIGNS

DOT-FILLED SQUARES

LINEAR FILL-IN

CONTRASTING GEOMETRY

MOTIF REPEAT

DOT-AND-BALL COMBINATIONS

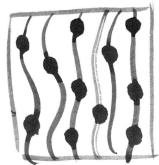

DOTTING THE LINE

DOTS AND LINES

STRING OF SPOTS

FOLIAGE/PLANT MOTIFS

FOLIAGE DESIGNS BASED ON VERTICAL LINES

FERNS AND TENDRILS

WHERE TO DECORATE?

This thought should be given consideration while making and designing—the two work in conjunction. Which pattern and where to put it for maximum effect (to enhance the pot) are the fundamental issues of surface design. Your decision may be influenced in part by the choice of decorating medium—for example, a complicated shape won't take kindly to a blanket-style stencil, and a tall straight vase will prove difficult to decorate with trailed slips. While on the subject, may I remind you again that the more complicated the pot, the harder it is to decorate because there are more visual elements to balance.

Planning out your design on the pot will help you economize on mistakes. With a blunt stick or lightly drawn pencil marks, you should locate the placement and spacing of the design. It need not be copied in great detail, just enough to reassure you that it fits the form without compromise. Doing so will mean one less thing to worry about. Be aware that technique and materials have a huge bearing on the character of a pattern. Try this as an exercise: Take one simple design and, using three different glazing or coloring techniques, apply it to three similar pots. The resulting pots should have very different personalities! A note of assurance: With few exceptions, failed attempts can be washed off and the pot dried out before you start again. Slips can be wiped off with a rubber rib, and, so long as the pot doesn't get too saturated, a second or third attempt should be possible.

Where the design is placed will also alter your perception of the piece. Blanketing a pot with decoration—particularly a complicated form like a teapot—can be overkill. Train your eye; look at other potters' pots to see how they tackled design issues. Patterns and decoration can be used more effectively when used selectively. Here are some sketches to show how a pot can be divided into zones for decorating. The shaded areas and subtle change in decoration show how the placement of pattern or color can drastically alter the visual weight and overall feel of a piece. Note how the horizontal white center band in the second sketch increases the fullness of the form. Contours, height, and width can all be exaggerated to your advantage. A pot may appear lighter by decorating the upper section, and more weighty in reverse. Aim to exploit some of these principles in order to give more impact to your decoration.

THE RULE OF THIRDS

This is not so much a rule but something to consider and decide whether it's suitable for your particular design needs. It can be helpful if you're really stuck about where to put your marks! The thirds rule divides the pot into three equal, horizontal (possibly vertical) sections. The three zones can be used to help place your design to maximum effect. The following sketches show some of the ways it can be utilized. There's something classic and honest about these proportions; they loosen the symmetrical framework that can often be so rigid.

EMILY SCHROEDER WILLIS Emily holds an M.F.A. from the University of Colorado in Boulder. She is the recipient of numerous awards and scholarships, including a Jerome Fellowship from the Northern Clay Center and a Sage Scholarship from the Archie Bray Foundation. She has exhibited her work in Europe, Central America, Australia, and throughout the United States. She has been an artist-in-residence at the Archie Bray Foundation in Helena, Montana, the Zentrum für Keramik in Berlin, Germany, and the Alberta College of Art and Design in Alberta, Canada. Emily has a studio in Chicago. To see more of her work, go to http://emilyschroeder.com.

A *PINK FLOWER BRICK*, 2012, 7$\frac{1}{2}$ x 5$\frac{1}{2}$" (19 x 14 cm), porcelain **B** *PINK AND WHITE PLATE*, 2012, 1 x 9" (2.5 x 22.9 cm), porcelain **C** *GRAY PITCHER*, 2012, 10 x 6" (25.4 x 15.2 cm), porcelain **D** *LOBED VASE*, 2012, 9$\frac{1}{2}$ x 9 x 5" (24.1 x 22.9 x 12.7 cm), porcelain **E** *WHITE LOBED VASE*, 2012, 8 x 8 x 3" (20.3 x 20.3 x 7.6 cm), porcelain **F** *CUP #20*, 2012, 3 x 3" (7.6 x 7.6 cm), porcelain **G** *WHITE CREAM AND SUGAR SET*, 2012, 3 x 5$\frac{1}{2}$ x 2" (7.6 x 14 x 5 cm) each, porcelain

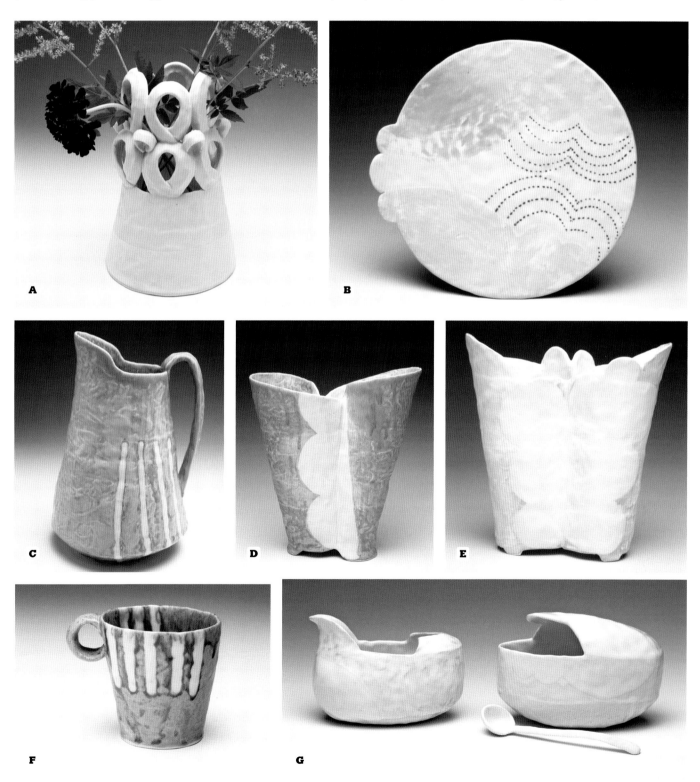

VASE OF MANY FACES

Without embellishments this vase is a simple, unassuming form. It has good proportions and a pleasing overall shape. To glaze it in one color would suffice. Its uncluttered simplicity would allow it to wear any shade of glaze. But for the decorator, this kind of blank shape—one devoid of fussy details—offers tremendous potential, as it's essentially a three-dimensional canvas. Scope of this sort of decorating freedom need not be limited to vases—a bowl or a simple covered jar could have the same potential. The point to remember is this: the more detailed and complicated the form, the more limited your choice for decoration. A spout, a handle, a florid rim, as wonderful as they are, they all become elements that must be considered when planning your surface design and therefore create surface decoration limitations. This vase is the antithesis of all that!

Here it is with six different finishes illustrating that its universal form allows great scope for color and decoration. This is not a finite series by any means, just a handful of examples of what is possible. Notice how the character of the piece is greatly altered depending on the style, scale, and color of surface treatment.

Vertical and horizontal stripes can be used in various widths, maximizing or minimizing their impact and creating exciting illusions. Bold, wide stripes tend to lend a more humorous air, whereas thinner ones generally have a more serious tone (think clowns versus pinstripe suits!). Finer, horizontal bands as seen with vase [E], emphasize the curves of the form compared to that of the bold vertical stripes on vase [F], which have a comical boldness that exaggerate the vase's height, as well as having a more flattening effect.

The vase with the thin vertical grooves and matt turquoise glaze has a different character altogether, its treatment being more restrained than the other linear examples. Generally, dull surfaces are more serious than shiny ones, so this vase is more sober in tone [G].

The vase's simple shape and smooth surface invite freer modes of decorating such as in the expressionistic colored brush strokes and drips of vase [H]. The vigorous marks do not necessarily echo the curves of the form and although spontaneous, they are carefully considered so as to harmonize with the abstract form of the vase. The three contrasting colors add to the dramatic nature of the brushwork.

Color also plays a role in vase [I]. As with clothing, darker colors are more serious, bright colors more frivolous. The red confetti vase would have been quite a different character if the glaze colors were in shades of gray.

Surface texture can also be exploited. This chocolate brown vase with its flaky, rippling surface repels and attracts all at once. Enhanced surface modeling moves the vase into a sculptural domain—another exciting area of study [J].

CLAYS

There are three main categories or classifications of clay body: earthenware, stoneware, and porcelain. This grouping is based mainly on the differing firing temperatures of these clays, but also on the clays' distinct handling qualities. With the exception of porcelain, within each group there are many "flavors," ranging in color and texture. It's imperative that, before you begin making a piece, you select the correct clay for the kind of glaze you want. For instance, if you want to use a speckled stoneware glaze, you wouldn't choose a red earthenware clay.

White clays yield brighter colors, just as white paper does. If you don't have a white or pale clay body, you can always apply a layer of white slip to mask the darker color beneath, giving the impression of a lighter clay. As with all slips, application must be made just before the leather-hard stage.

EARTHENWARE

These are low-firing clay bodies with a temperature range of approximately 1830–2156°F (1000–1180°C). The more traditional and commonly used is a dark reddish brown clay called "red earthenware" or "red terra cotta"; it may or may not have grog. It's a terrific hand-building clay with good plastic strength, and generally fires to a warm, toasted orange. There are now buff and gray colored earthenware clays, specially formulated to become more dense and semi vitrified at lower temperatures, though the clay is likely to be porous without the coating of a glaze. Earthenware has a lightness to it, making it markedly less strong than the denser, high-fired stoneware.

White earthenware clays are useful for inlay work, their bright neutral bases allowing the oxide or stain to give the clearest color response. Hand building with white earthenwares can present difficulties in construction; being ultra smooth, these clays although slippery, lack plastic strength and often prove difficult to join.

STONEWARE

This is the broadest category of clays, with many different colors—including white, cream, gray, buff, pink, and brown—and textures available. They're mixed to a variety of textures; some that are used for sculptural work are extremely coarse. They generally have excellent workability and plastic strength, and can be fired from 2190–2380°F (1200–1300°C). These higher temperatures cause the clay to become dense and hard—hence the name, stoneware. Because the clay becomes vitrified, it's nonporous, even without a glaze. Some stoneware is specially formulated for use in electric or gas kiln firings. With the interest in low-temperature stoneware (cone 6), manufacturers have developed clays that vitrify at the lower end of the temperature range, thus making them more compatible with the glaze and providing a better fit. Do check that you are buying the correct clay for your firing and glazing requirements. Read all the information provided by the manufacturer.

As with earthenware, a buff or dark-colored clay can be made to give a brighter glaze response with the application of a white slip.

PORCELAIN

The name has a certain prodigious allure, conjuring images of fine, delicate ceramics with a luminous alabaster quality. Porcelain certainly is a unique clay, with a pure, ultra-smooth texture, super plasticity, and a warm, white, milky tone that seems to absorb and reflect light all at once. You either love it or hate it. Some people find it slimy and temperamental; to others its creamy sensuousness is addictive. For hand building, in fact, for pinching especially, it really is worth trying. It can be brought to a more extreme thinness quickly and without the need of any tools. Refining of the surface should be carried out when the clay is bone dry (wear a dust mask); any sooner and every scrape will show as an ugly facet. Of course, a delicate touch is needed at this stage to not crack the wafer-thin form—and it's thinness that you should aspire to, as this will reveal its other unique characteristic: its fired translucent, glass-like quality. It's a delight to carve and responds to sgraffito like no other clay.

The only difficulty with pinching porcelain is the joining process. You cannot hope for a soft handle to stay put if attached to a leather-hard pot. For two elements to unite and stay united, they must be brought together when at exactly the same stage of dryness and softness. Handles are best formed, shaped, and left to stiffen before being stuck in place with slip. Even then it may be touch and go. Joining while clay is still soft is the surest way to get a good bond, but, as with the handle attachment, this isn't always possible.

Porcelain makes glazes sing. Traditionally, transparent and semi-transparent glazes were used, as these enhance the light-absorbing qualities. But there are potters who use darker, more opaque colors, as the porcelain makes such a fine and irresistible canvas for color.

Porcelain demands to be fired at the highest of stoneware temperatures. Try 2372°F (1300°C) or even a little beyond. The high firing temperature causes vitrification, as the particles within the clay melt together to form a dense, impervious, glass-like quality.

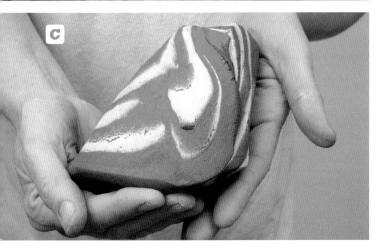

Marbling Colored Clays

Imagine a pot that looks like marble cake! This is the kind of effect you get when you mix two differently colored clays together. In fact, you can mix several different hues to get all kinds of interesting effects.

Only combine clays of the same kind (i.e., earthenware with earthenware) so that they shrink together. When you're ready to combine the colored clays, you must not knead them too much or the colors will become muddied. Best results are from clay colors that have high contrast. For example, a simple and striking combination is red and white earthenware mixed together. You could do the same with a light and dark stoneware combination.

Your color palette expands and gets really exciting when you start to color your own clay. Use a white one as a base—porcelain is the purest—for a brighter color response (like mixing into white paint). Oxides and stains can be easily wedged into soft clay, making it possible to have shades of blue, green, yellow, purple, gray, and other colors. You'll find mixing techniques on the opposite page and recipes in back of the book.

1   The simplest way to combine your clays is to make a sandwich. Slice off wedges of colored clay, layering them as if making an extravagant sandwich [A]. As you lay one down on top of another, try not to trap air.

2   When you have a stack, slam and slap the layers together to make a block shape. Clean up the edges by trimming off irregularities [B], and pat the clay firmly into a ball that's ready for pinching.

3   A variation of this sandwiching is to knead the clay two or three times before shaping the clay into a ball. This will cause the different colors to swirl together, creating a more marbled effect [C].

4   Think carefully before sticking in your thumb. Do you want the stripes of clay running horizontally? Vertically? Diagonally? Cutting and reassembling the sandwich can give some wonderfully complex results [D].

An alternative is to place chunks of shaped, colored clay on the outside of a clay ball, slapping them hard so that they bed firmly in (as was done with the Triplet Herb Planter, page 88). As you pinch the pot, the colored pieces will spread and envelope the form, almost like an inlay. This method allows you to create a more controlled patterned surface.

In all instances, the marbling and layering of colors will be more crisp and vivid if the surface of the clay is shaved and smoothed when the clay has reached a good, stiff, leather-hard firmness; if done earlier, the colors will smudge. So long as there's sufficient contrast between the clays, you will not need to glaze the piece. However, as with colored slips, a clear glaze will moisten the hue like water on a wet pebble. The inside can be glazed for practical purposes.

Coloring Clay

Adding stain or oxide to clay would be suitable for making colored clay for inlay and for use in the sandwich marbling technique shown on page 70. The idea is to make batches of single colored clay(s) to your own specification. A greater and subtler color palette is possible by mixing oxides or stains into a white or off-white clay. Keeping your base clay pale will allow for greater color intensity as it will not be muddied by the oxides already present in the clay (most commonly iron oxide). Making a small batch for inlay is quick and easy, but more time and effort will be needed if you require a large amount for marbling.

Recipes for colors and proportions are in the back of the book (page 123).

Round off a ball of moist clay and use your thumb to form a well in the center [E]. Pour about half a teaspoon of water, along with the appropriate amount of stain/oxide into the hole (the more oxide or stain that you use, the more you will need to add). Let the oxide soak into the water.

Carefully press the sides of the ball together and slowly squeeze and seal the opening—this bit will be wonderfully gooey [F]!

Begin the kneading process. Roll the clay between the palms of your hands to make a sausage shape [G], squash it back into a ball, and then repeat the movement; do this several times. Unless you have a particularly large ball of clay, don't be tempted to roll it on the table, as you will lose some of the color.

Continue the rolling and squashing process until the color graining becomes more even [H]. Basically the more you knead, the more even the color will be. If the clay starts to look or feel dry, give it a quick spritz with a water sprayer. Keep the colored clay in a plastic bag clearly labeled with the type of clay, colorant, and percentage used.

JENNY MENDES Jenny holds a B.F.A. from Washington University in St. Louis, Missouri. Her ceramic artwork has been exhibited nationally at galleries and juried shows. She has participated in artist residencies in France, Slovenia, Macedonia, and the United States. A full-time studio artist since 1994, she lives in Chesterland, Ohio. Her web site is www.jennymendes.com.

A *MONKEY BOY*, 2012, 3³/₄" (9.5 cm) dia. x 1¹/₂" (3.8 cm), high   **B** and **C** *COLLECTION OF BOWLS* **D** *3 BIRDS*, 2012, 3¹/₂" (8.9 cm) dia. x 1¹/₂" (3.8 cm) high **E** *PINCH*, 2012, 3¹/₂" (8.9 cm) dia. x 1¹/₂" (3.8 cm) high **F** *SHE BUG*, 2012, 3" (7.6 cm) dia. x 1¹/₂" (3.8 cm) high **G** *LUCKY CATCH*, 2012, 3³/₄" (9.5 cm) dia. x 1¹/₄" (3.2 cm) high **H** *MAGIC EGG*, 2012, 4" (10.2 cm) dia. x 1¹/₄" (3.2 cm) high **I** *DOG DANCE*, 2012, 3¹/₄" (8.3 cm) dia. x 1¹/₂" (3.8 cm) high

A

C

B

D

E

F

G

H

I

KILNS & GLAZE FIRINGS

Kilns come in all shapes and sizes and can be fueled with various combustibles and heat sources. Wood, oil, sawdust, gas, and electricity are among the most common. In some parts of the world, low-temperature firings are even carried out using dried animal dung or grass! For the purposes of this book, electric and gas fired are the two types of kilns that most potters are likely to come across or have access to, so those are the types I'll discuss.

All glazes must be fired in a kiln to melt onto the pot. There are several kinds of firings, ranging in temperature and kiln atmosphere, each yielding or possessing their own distinctive qualities.

KILN TYPES

Kilns are similar to domestic ovens in that they are generally either electric or gas, though other types of solid fuel can be used. However, the similarity stops there. Kitchen ovens can only heat up to 550°F (290°C). A kiln used for firing clay needs a minimum of 1800°F (980°C). Like new cars, the sizes and shapes of kilns vary enormously and there are many to choose from. Also like purchasing a vehicle, you can get an upgrade by adding options, but of course the price will increase accordingly.

Gas

Used mostly by professional potters and commonly found at communal craft and art centers, these kinds of kilns are fueled either by natural gas or propane. They need not be large, but they're entirely manual and should only be fired by a practitioner who understands the firing process. Most potters choose to work with gas kilns because they want the benefit of controlling the atmosphere in the kiln—this can't be done with an electric kiln. Decreasing the oxygen level in the kiln causes an imbalance in the combustion of carbon, thus creating reduction atmosphere. This has a huge impact on the color of some glazes and clay bodies, giving a warmth and depth just not possible in an oxidized firing. With reduction firings, there are flames and smoke and carbon monoxide—so adequate ventilation is paramount! These types of kilns should not be sited within the main workshop, but have their own room or covered outdoor space.

Electric

This is the most common type of kiln used by potters. They're convenient to fire, relatively easy to install, and can run for years without needing maintenance. Electric kilns can only be used for bisque and oxidized glaze firings. The atmosphere in the kiln is clean and smokeless (though there can still be a smell and fumes.) The consistency of this atmosphere means that glazing results won't be susceptible to tremendous variation.

Another advantage of choosing an electric kiln is that they can be programmed to carry out a firing, allowing you to get on with other things. These computer programs are so sophisticated you can delay-start the firing. These kiln accessories are costly and will substantially increase the cost of your equipment. Manual electric kilns are perfectly adequate; they're just more hands on. I've had many a late night waiting to turn up the heat dials on a kiln! Most

electric kilns will shut off using the fail-safe kiln sitter device, which is very convenient and simple to use. In fact, your kiln won't start unless the kiln sitter prong has been activated. Your kiln manual will show you how to set it up.

Kiln sizes vary enormously, from shoebox sized to those the size of a large closet—literally a walk-in kiln! They can be top or front loading, round, square, or oval. Your choice of kiln will be a personal one based on practical factors such as space and cost. I was always advised to buy the biggest kiln you can afford, as even then, it'll never be big enough. You never know what you may want to make a few years from now.

Electric kilns fire to different temperatures. Be sure to study all the manufacturer's information, as this will tell you the maximum firing temperature of each particular kiln. If cone 6 is stated as the maximum, it'll mean you can never glaze at high-fire stoneware temperatures.

Electric kilns are generally considered indoor kilns, which means they must be sited with care. They're usually placed on a tiled or concrete floor (I use large patio slabs), and the walls around them protected with special heat-resistant sheetrock. Adequate ventilation must be provided while the kiln is being fired. Although no carbon fuel is involved, all firings emit fumes from organic matter in the clay and chemicals within the glaze. Some of these fumes can be toxic, but generally they're just unpleasant. Kiln fans and chimney hoods are sold as kiln accessories that solve this ventilation problem. These extractors will also whisk away much of the heat that can make a small room insufferable to work in. For smaller kilns, I think it's sufficient to ventilate a room by opening a couple of windows and perhaps using a simple window and ceiling fan to aid air circulation.

Most electric kilns have hefty plugs and energy needs not usually available in a domestic situation. For these reasons, an electrical upgrade is likely to be in order—the bigger the kiln, the more energy required. Before purchasing, check with an electrician to confirm that the premises you are working on are suitably wired to accommodate your intended kiln.

TYPES OF FIRINGS

Earthenware (Cone 04 - 3)

This has a broad firing range: 1922–2106°F (1050–1152°C). It's usually carried out in an electric kiln. This is considered low-temperature glazing, and the glazes have a softer, less-dense feel to them. Also, the clay may not necessarily be vitrified, resulting in a less-tight bond between glaze and clay body. The advantages of earthenware firing are the bright color palette of glazes and the decorating possibilities. There's also an economic benefit to this lower temperature firing. Suitable traditional clays are red and white earthenware, but your pottery supplier may recommend other plastic clay bodies.

Stoneware

There are three types of stoneware firings.

MID-TEMPERATURE STONEWARE

Mid-temperature stoneware firings range from cone 4 through cone 7 with temperatures running 2134–2219°F (1164–1215°C). More potters are turning to this lower stoneware firing in order to reduce fuel costs. There's a range of clays on the market that are specifically developed to mature (vitrify) at these temperatures, allowing for greater compatibility between clay and glaze, and making it less likely to chip. Traditionally, electric stoneware firings have a limited color palette, one that's more subdued than that of earthenware or reduction-fired stoneware. However, developments in glaze formulations have widened the color selection in commercially prepared glazes.

HIGH TEMPERATURE OXIDIZED STONEWARE

Similar to mid stoneware but producing denser, more vitrified ware, high temperature oxidized stoneware firings consist of cones 8–11, with temperatures of 2257–2365°F (1236–1300°C). Clays can be white, buff, or porcelain. Again, colors are more subdued and earthy. Many commercially prepared stains (particularly reds, pinks, oranges, and some yellows) are unstable at this temperature, though there are now some bright colors available that'll endure this temperature (check labeling on materials). The atmosphere in the kiln is clean and smoke free, as high levels of oxygen are present in the kiln during the firing cycle.

HIGH-TEMPERATURE STONEWARE REDUCTION

Like high temperature oxidized stoneware, high temperature stoneware reduction firings (in gas, wood, or oil-fired kilns) include cones 8–11, reaching temperatures of 2257-2365°F (1236–1300°C), but in this volatile and thrilling firing, the oxygen intake into the kiln is restricted, creating a carbon-izing (carbon monoxide) atmosphere. Many oxides go through dramatic color changes due to this oxygen-starved atmosphere—copper may turn from green to red! The color of the clay reacts to the atmosphere, too; any iron-bearing bodies will deepen in color and may speckle on the surface. Porcelain is very at home in this kind of firing, and there's a wide choice of clay colors and textures developed especially for the process. It's a spectacular thing to see a reduction firing in process. Many pottery centers run workshops in which they offer this of kind of firing (carried out by a professional) for finished work. It's certainly something I recommend you look out for.

Kilns and Glaze Firings

There is one delightfully small kiln that I find enormously beneficial and practical. Often called a test kiln, it can be plugged into a regular household 120v outlet (see bottom photo on the opposite page). It's light, compact, and portable. Some models have a strong, lightweight detachable stand, which fits nicely over a single patio slab—or half a dozen bricks. The kiln chamber is large enough to fire a small teapot, a mug, or a couple of bowls. For a potter not trying to produce quantity, but perhaps just a few things for their own domestic use, this kind of kiln would be ideal. I can fit about seven large glaze tests in mine, and the kiln itself will fire to up to cone 10. Many of the pieces in this book were fired in this kiln. I was even able to load, fire, and unpack all in the same day, as the kiln fires rapidly and cools quickly. It's a simple manual kiln with one dial that controls the amount of heat going into the kiln. The inside dimensions of mine are 8 x 8 x 9 inches (20.3 x 20.3 x 22.9 cm), but this will vary according to the manufacturer. All good pottery suppliers will stock them.

could be a
/cocoa shaker?

e/w
white
slip honey
glaze

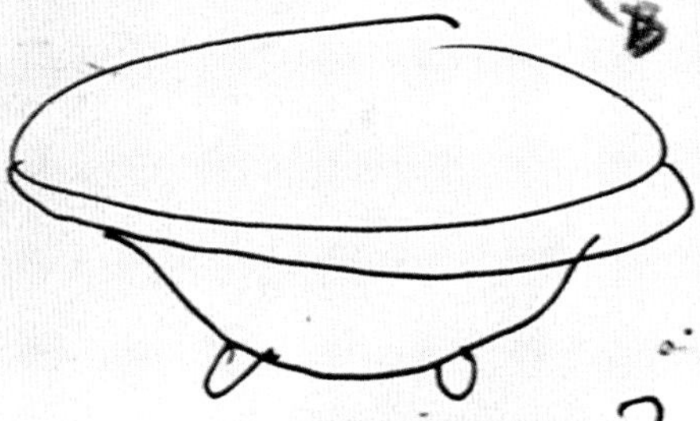

Bowls

#2

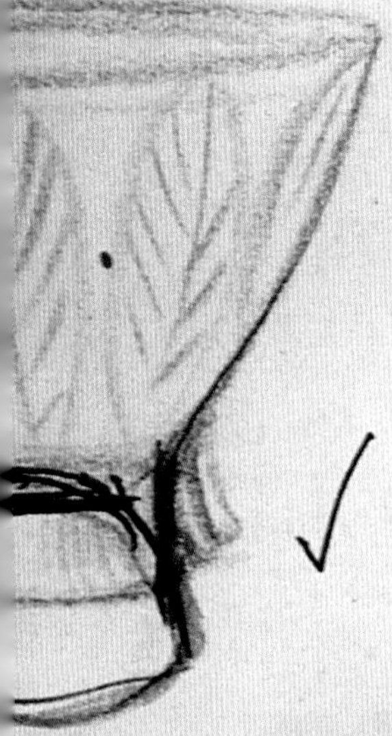

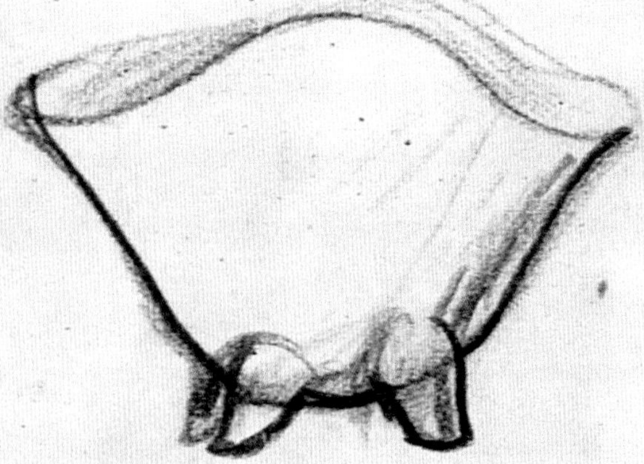

marbled?

wax or
resist leaves

oxids.

✓

swoopy.

ridges - tin glaze

Honey +
white slip?

#4

coarse stoneware
or
white tin glaze
o/e/w.

Pressed
inde
wigg

? Ca
Ri

applied
ridges.

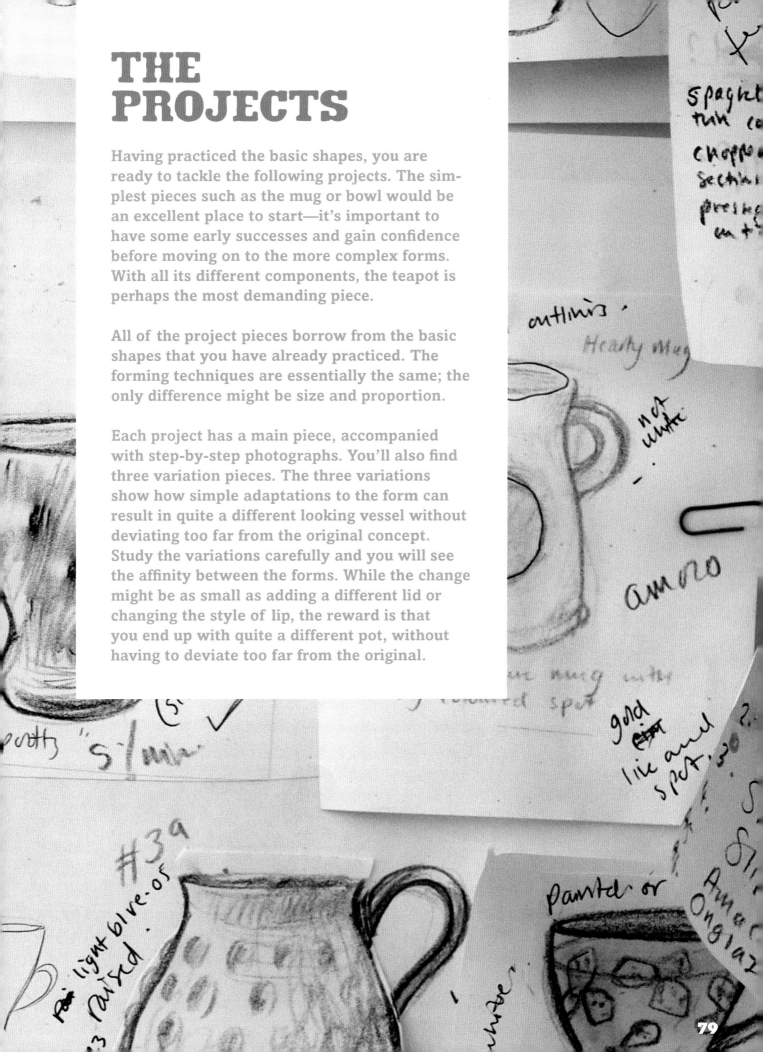

THE PROJECTS

Having practiced the basic shapes, you are ready to tackle the following projects. The simplest pieces such as the mug or bowl would be an excellent place to start—it's important to have some early successes and gain confidence before moving on to the more complex forms. With all its different components, the teapot is perhaps the most demanding piece.

All of the project pieces borrow from the basic shapes that you have already practiced. The forming techniques are essentially the same; the only difference might be size and proportion.

Each project has a main piece, accompanied with step-by-step photographs. You'll also find three variation pieces. The three variations show how simple adaptations to the form can result in quite a different looking vessel without deviating too far from the original concept. Study the variations carefully and you will see the affinity between the forms. While the change might be as small as adding a different lid or changing the style of lip, the reward is that you end up with quite a different pot, without having to deviate too far from the original.

BIG BOWL

The bowl is an infinitely useful object and a pleasing shape to make. The addition of the tall, stemlike foot lends a more stately quality. Try experimenting with the proportions by enlarging or reducing the size of each element—for instance, a big bowl with a shorter foot or a smaller bowl with a taller foot. The resulting pieces will be dramatically different.

Pinch It

1 This bowl is quite large, so begin with a 5-1b. (2.27 kg) lump of soft clay. Shape it into a ball, then pinch it open large enough to comfortably fit your fist inside. The base of this chunky pinch pot must be kept quite thick during the early forming stage [A].

2 Raise your arm and slap the sides of the pot downward toward your elbow. Turn your fist so that all sides of the clay get the slapping treatment [B]. Keep your arm more horizontal to prevent the opening from getting too narrow. Your goal is to establish a good height before widening out the general form. Don't thin the rim at this point. Continue slapping and shaping until you feel the clay needs to rest and stiffen up. Sit it rim-side down on plastic.

3 For the second stage of shaping, I like to rest the pot in my lap; that way I can better gauge the thicknesses and the strength of the clay and have a more tactile relationship with it. Start to press out the base of the bowl (careful not to puncture!), which is more pointed than rounded. To create the subtle curve of the form, let your inside hand do most of the shaping, pressing, stroking, and stretching of the clay outward [C]. Keep a close eye on the profile of the bowl, checking to see where it needs more work. The widening of the bowl will stretch the rim thinner; don't pinch it unless it seems overly chunky. You'll thin it later. If you try it now it can crack. Let the form rest again and then continue with the shaping. You should repeat this sequence several times. I cannot stress enough how important the resting stages are in managing large open forms—they're the key to success! Try to develop as much of the clay into the bowl form as possible, meaning, make the clay go as far as you can in order to get the biggest bowl possible. When you're satisfied with the form, rest it rim-side down.

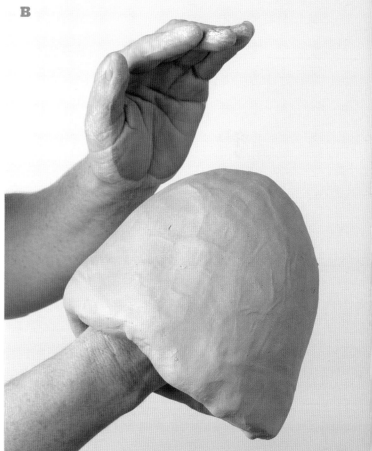

4 The foot should be about one-third of the pot's form and quite chunky, so use a pound (.45 kg) of clay. Pinch the ball of clay into a deep bowl shape with inward-curving sides. Keep the rim and the bottom area quite thick. Observe the proportion and adjust the foot taller and wider as needed.

5 Puncture through the pinch pot foot to make it into a collar shape. Give both ends an outward flare, being careful that the clay doesn't get too thin [D]. The newly opened end is the part that will join to the base of the bowl. Let it firm up so that it's as stiff as the bowl.

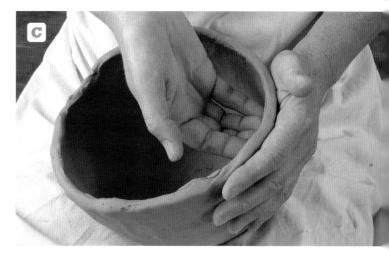

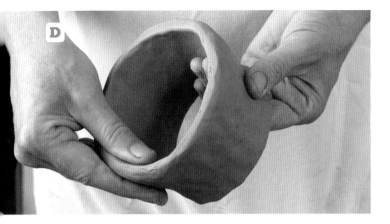

6 Trim the rim of the foot if it's uneven. Sit the bowl on the foot, turning it on a banding wheel to check if it's centered and level [E]. Use a stick to mark around the area where the foot will join the bowl, then apply slip to both the bowl and the foot.

7 Reassemble the two shapes, pressing the bowl firmly onto the foot. Give it a slight twist so that it locks in. Wipe away any oozing slip. Use your fingers to spread clay from the foot ring upwards onto the bowl [F]. Turn the piece over (use the double board technique if it's easier) and work the clay from inside the foot ring over the base of the bowl. While the bowl is upside down, reinforce the inside seam with a soft coil of clay. Depending on the softness of the clay and the weight of the piece, you may want to leave it like this for a while to dry out. The foot must be strong enough to support the bowl without squashing.

8 Turn the bowl upside down and use slip and a soft coil of clay to reinforce the outside seam. Bear in mind that this coil may be thicker, as you want to integrate these two shapes, giving the impression of one. Take time to check the overall shape. You should still be able to manipulate the clay, but be gentle. Pinch the rim thinner if it looks too thick, and, if necessary, trim it level [G].

9 As the bowl stiffens up, further refining of the surface can be carried out both inside and out. Use toothed tools and ribs to even out the surface. Once it's leather hard, trim the rim of the bowl to make it level and smooth away any sharp edges.

10 Make a 45° undercut at the outside edge of the foot ring. This provides the visual lift a bowl like this deserves. Arbuckle Tin glaze with wax resist detail and colored onglaze decoration.

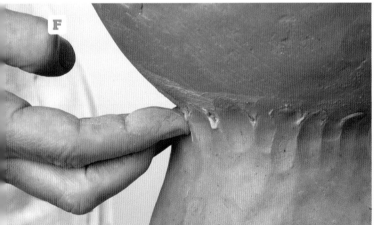

WAVY EDGE BOWL Keeping a similar shape, the rim is turned slightly outward. When leather-hard, the rim was trimmed level and cut to give a wave effect. It has a "doughnut" foot. Reduction fired stoneware with Caribbean Green glaze.

SCOOPED BOWL The original bowl shape is formed deeper and wider. While the clay's still soft, press two opposite sides inward using the palms of your hands; this will encourage a more oval shape. The pot on the left is made in the same way as the one on the right except glazed on the inside with Arbuckle Tin glaze and with Guild Honey on the outside. Both bowls have leaf stencils. The bowl on the right is glazed inside and out with Suzi's Glossy Honey.

WIDE DISH-BOWL Pinched wider and flatter, the original bowl shape is stretched out to become a platter. The edge left natural and untrimmed, it is raised up on three well-spaced nodule feet. Brush decorated with turquoise and white slips, transparent earthenware glaze, gold and mother-of-pearl commercial lustres.

COVERED JAR

This is a large and roomy jar based on a traditional country design. It can be made at any scale, but the bigger version gives more storage options, such as for rice or flour. Make sure you have a well-fitting lid and strong handles for easy lifting.

Pinch It

1 As this will be quite a substantial piece, pinch off two 3-lb. (1.4 kg) lumps of clay. Pinch both lumps open and then shape them over your fist. You're aiming for two deep, flared bowls.

2 Join one rim to the other. Then paddle and shape the profile.

3 With the piece placed on a banding wheel, cut out a circular opening at the neck; make the opening slightly smaller than you need; it can be trimmed back later [A]. You should be able to get your hand inside, so take this opportunity to smooth out the inside joining seam. You can also swell out the shape if necessary. If the pot feels vulnerable and soft, let it firm up before proceeding.

4 Flatten the base by giving it a few firm taps on the table. Turn the form over (remember, it must be strong enough to support its own weight!) and attach a foot ring made from a generous coil of soft clay. Smooth in the join both inside and out. Stand it up to check that it's level, then turn it back over so that the foot ring can firm up.

5 Use another soft, flattened coil of clay to make the lip of the pot. Take your time getting this right. Even slight changes in height and width will alter the look of the pot [B].

6 Once the lip is attached, trim away from inside any part that interrupts the opening. Smooth in the seams inside and out, then check from above that the lip is still circular [C].

7 The lid is a wide-flaring cone with a turned-out rim [D]. Use the calipers to help gauge the diameter and shape the lid in stages. Trim the upper surface of the pot's

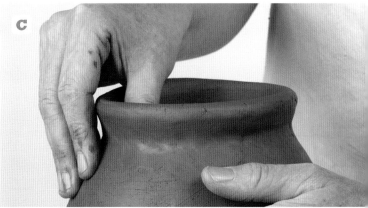

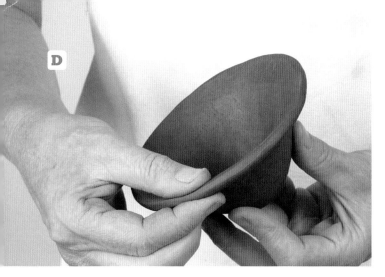

rim so that it's flat. The lid's rim should sit neatly and closely on this surface—the tighter the seal, the more practical your jar will be for food storage. When the lid is strong enough, flatten a coil and add it to the inside of the lid's rim. This is the flange that'll hold the lid in place [E].

8 Place the lid onto the pot. To make the knob, slip and join a log-shaped chunk of clay to the lid top. With wet fingers, twist and twirl the clay while turning the pot on the banding wheel [F]. Flatten the top of the knob with a few swift pats of the paddle. You could take the lid off the pot and mold it that way, but I like to see the entire form while the knobbed lid is being added—it helps establish the correct scale.

9 Work the surface of the pot, shaving away any nasty bumps and textures.

10 Time for the handles. It's always best to make them together so there's more chance of making a matching pair! But remember, however much you strive, your handles aren't likely to be truly symmetrical—this should be seen as a virtue and a characteristic of all handmade pottery. Roll out two very soft coils of clay and cut them to the same length. Flatten them.

11 Mark the position of the first handle, then slip and join it, pressing one end in first before bending the clay strap over and thumbing it in the other end [G].

12 Mark the position of the second handle, checking its location from several angles The best handles have a fluid, natural look. If they don't look right, don't waste time fiddling with them; take them off and start again.

13 Make a beveled undercut around the base of the pot. This softens the edge of the foot and gives a visual lift to the piece.

14 When the entire form is leather hard, use a wire loop tool to carve out the horizontal grooves. Work with the pot on a banding wheel, gradually rotating the piece as you carve out the clay. If you prefer, you can carve the handles before joining but you must do it while the handle shapes are flat and soft, then bend them into the correct curve and leave to stiffen before joining. Fired to cone 5 (no glaze).

COVERED JAR WITH BUTTERFLY LID One large, inverted pinch pot forms the body of this simple, tapered jar, though you could make it from joining two halves. The decorative lid detail is made from two pinched disks of soft clay. High-fired reduction stoneware with Plum glaze.

VOLUPTUOUS CACTUS-COVERED JAR Two bowl-shaped pinch pots form the body, with a smaller version inverted for the bulbous outsized lid. A deep gallery and flange holds the lid securely in place. The raised texture is applied when leather hard. Fired to cone 6 with Amaco PC2 Sturation Gold.

PIE CRUST-COVERED JAR The two original pinch pots are stretched out to make a taller, narrower vessel. After the opening is cut out, a generous coil is added and crimped to give a piecrust edge. The simple convex dish lid has a high arching loop handle. High-fired reduction stoneware with Cushing Matt glaze.

TRIPLET HERB PLANTER

Perfect for a sunny windowsill. If you extend the number of compartments, add extra pairs of feet to the middle pots for more support. If you're not comfortable pinching each sphere as a whole, then construct each pot using the composite method of two joined bowls, cutting each one open when it's leather hard.

Pinch It

1 Weigh out three similarly sized lumps of clay. I chose to embellish my pieces with soft clays of contrasting color—white earthenware used in its pure state and some colored with about 2% red iron oxide. This resulted in a decorative surface design that by its nature has a pleasing organic rhythm. Prepare several small balls of the colored clay and arrange them over the surface of your main ball of clay. Pat them firmly into the surface so that they flatten and unite with the clay beneath. Now begin the pinching process as for a sphere. Keep the opening narrow and the walls an even thickness [A]. As you shape each ball, compare their size and shape against each other. They need not be identical, but strive for similarity. When the spheres start to get too floppy and unmanageable, rest them on their rims to firm up.

2 Before the spheres get too stiff, continue to enlarge and refine them. Small stroking movements inside with your fingertips will swell the curve, and a paddle used deftly on the outside will tighten up the profile. However, only use the paddle if necessary, as the idea is to eliminate any bumps.

3 Tooling and smoothing the surface should be carried out when the spheres are almost leather hard. Trim the rims level before joining the flared lips.

4 Roll a soft coil of clay for the rim. Slip the top edge and outer rim of one pot. Press one end of the coil to the outside, uppermost edge. Rotate the pot, thumbing in the coil at the bottom to secure the join [B]. Try not to squeeze the top part of the coil; it should project straight upwards from the pot.

5 Smooth the seam on the outside of the pot. Support the inside wall with your fingertips and smooth the inside seam. Work quickly so that the coil doesn't start to dry out.

6 Between your thumb and forefinger, gently pinch the soft coil to heighten and thin it [C]. Small, repeated movements will help keep it level.

7 With the clay between your thumb and forefinger, and held at a low horizontal position, angle the rim gently outward [D]. If the clay is too dry, it may start to show small cracks. A feeding of water from your fingertip (run it around the rim a few times) will help keep them at bay. Take care and don't make it too soggy or it'll get very slimy! Check from above that the opening is still circular. Let the pots rest.

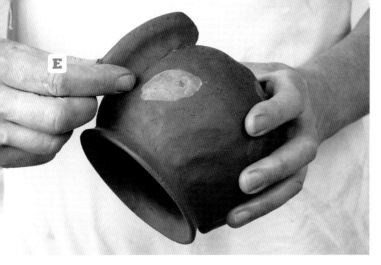

If the rims are strong enough, you can simply turn them upside down. Otherwise, use the nest supports. Wrap the main body shapes in plastic; they must not dry beyond leather hard.

8 When the rims are as firm as the bodies, trim away any projecting clay from inside each rim and fill the shallow crevices with slip and a soft coil of clay. Study the outside shape and surface. Any last minute shaping or scraping should be done now.

9 Line up the three pots, each one resting on its rim. With a knife or stick, mark the points where they'll join. These'll be at the widest parts of each sphere. The center pot will have a mark on two sides; the outer pots, just one mark each.

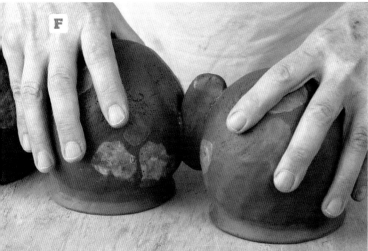

10 Making long, vertical smears, rub slip on the two joining areas of two of the pots. Roll a short coil and press a piece of it onto one of the slipped areas (it doesn't matter which one) [E]. The bigger you make this coil of clay, the greater the distance between the pots. Smooth it in all edges except the long, outer edge.

11 Brush some slip on the long outer edge and on the joining area of its awaiting partner pot. Keep them rim-side down while you work the join, blending it in between the two pots. Use a wooden modeling tool to help get between them [F].

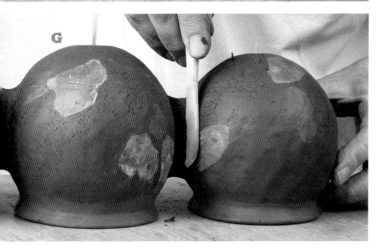

12 Repeat the same procedure with the last two pots (checking that all three pots are still set up in a straight line), adding the soft coil to one of them and pushing them together as you did before. Smooth in the join [G], but don't turn the group over. Cover the entire piece with plastic and let the connections firm up. Keep the piece upside down for the next stage.

13 To make the feet, roll out a coil to an even thickness and cut off four equal lengths; mine are about 1½ inches (3.8 cm). Don't make the feet too long and skinny or they'll be more vulnerable to breaking. Pinch or roll one end of each foot to a taper so that you have four stocky carrot shapes. Slice the fat joining ends to a 45° angle (approximately).

14 Mark off four joining areas on either side of the outer pots. The feet are set low and at the back end; notice how they grow out from the sides and aren't just stuck on underneath! Slip all the marked areas and the plump end of each foot. Lightly position each one, lining them up as equally as possible. They should all be sticking straight up. Take a good look from all sides to see if one is off kilter. Press each one at its base. It's important to get a good join, but don't over pinch and make it thin at the join point [H]. Keeping the foot thicker where it attaches gives visual strength. Turn the lower part of each foot outward so that it has a subtle kick. Let the feet dry out slowly until they're almost leather hard. Carefully turn the piece over to check that it's level. If any foot seems too long, turn the piece back over and trim the foot back with a sharp knife. While it dries, keep the piece upside down and lightly draped in plastic.

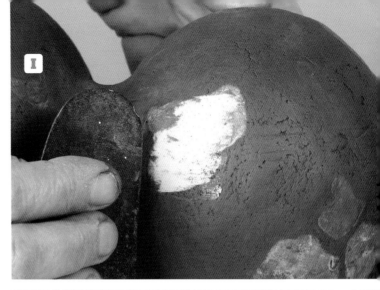

15 When the clay is leather hard, use the sharp edge of a steel rib or something similar to scrape down the surface; this will sharpen the contrast between the colored clays and help level out any unevenness in the contours of the pots [I].

16 Turn the piece upside down and pierce a drainage hole in the bottom of each pot, using a special hole-making tool [J]. Earthenware fired with Glossy Transparent glaze.

Many planters are left unglazed. In this condition, the clay is more porous so once planted, the surface will develop a pleasant patina from the salts and minerals leaching out of the soil and into the clay.

CRUSTY TERRA COTTA One large pinch-pot bowl is given a discreet doughnut foot—just enough to elevate. The surface is encrusted with balls of clay, smoothed in—but not too carefully—to give a tactile coarseness. Fired to cone 5 in an electric kiln. No glaze.

GILLED PLANTER This slightly taller pinch-pot bowl needs no extra foot elevation. When almost leather hard, strips of soft clay were applied in vertical bands, each one reaching up and over the lip to create an interesting edge. Reduction fired stoneware with Spoor Blue Slip Glaze.

FRINGE LIPPED PLANTER The lip of this simple bowl shape was cut with an old pair of scissors—do it before the clay is leather hard, then wiggle and move each frond to open up and animate. Manchester Tin Glaze over Black Slip. Scratched through before dry.

SHAKER

Not just for salt and pepper. Enlarge any one of these designs and you have a shaker fit to hold cinnamon, vanilla, sugar, cocoa—even talcum powder! To plug the hole underneath, you'll need a small, tapered cork. Craft shops sell various sizes, or you could try trimming down a wine cork using a sharp knife.

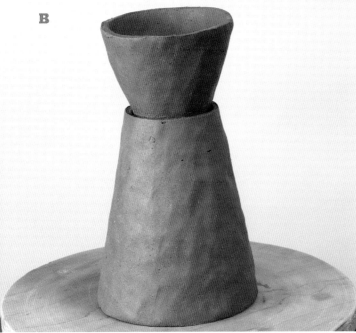

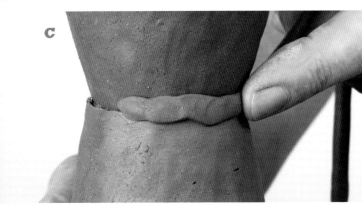

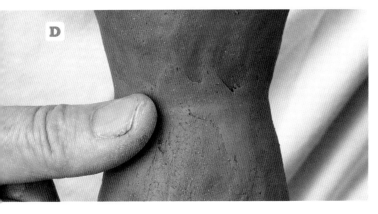

Pinch It

1 For one large shaker, weigh two balls of clay: one 6-oz (170 g) and one 4-oz (113 g) ball. The larger ball will become the shaker base and the smaller ball the top of the shaker. Keep the balls under plastic when you're not shaping them.

2 Pinch the 6-oz (170 g) ball into a gently tapered cone. Don't puncture through the other end just yet. Shape the cone by pinching and pulling to get as much length as possible, then poke through the base and pinch it longer and thinner.

3 When you have created the base cone, pinch the smaller ball in exactly the same way—forming the cone then piercing and pinching out the opposite end [A]. As you're working, check the size of this smaller shape against that of the larger to ensure that the proportion is pleasing. Let both shapes rest until they're firm enough to handle without them becoming misshapen.

4 Trim the larger cone so that the end is flat. Do the same with the smaller top piece, trimming the narrower end so that it inserts into the small opening of the large cone [B].

5 Apply slip to both shapes where they make contact, then assemble them, carefully pressing the seams together with thumb and forefinger. Cover the seam with a coil of clay and then smooth in [C & D].

6 Examine the overall shape for dimples or dents, gently pushing out the clay to help correct any unevenness. It's easiest to do this now before the piece becomes closed in. Check that the inside isn't too messy.

7 To make the flat ends that close the form, pinch two disks of clay—one smaller, and one larger. Press them onto a very smooth board or piece of cardboard so that they're smooth and flat. Let them dry to become the same firmness as the main shape.

8 Slip the wide end first. Apply slip to the bigger disk; guessing roughly where to paint the circle of slip. Carefully press the pot onto the disk, giving a little twist in one direction. You should feel it lock into the slip. It's worth giving a good tap on the table; this'll help compress the join. Trim around the base of each piece, cutting away the excess clay [E].

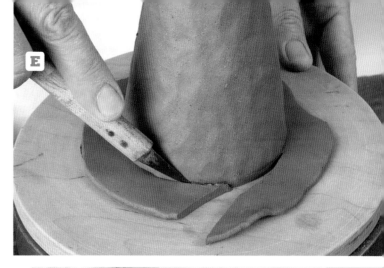

9 Join the smaller top disk in exactly the same way. When it's completely sealed in, go over the surface with a toothed-edged tool, scraping away bumps or lumps, then smooth the surface down with a rib.

10 Have your cork ready, as now is the time to cut the opening. Make a recess by tapping the center of the base. The clay should be soft enough to yield. Gradually it should recess into a large dimple. Make the indention wider by spreading out the tapping area, turning the piece as you go **[F]**. The recessed area needs to be wider than the cork and deep enough so that the cork doesn't project beyond the base. Use the end of the cork as a template to mark and then cut out a hole. Cut the hole a fraction wider to allow for shrinkage; the cork can always be trimmed or sanded for a tight fit.

11 Mark the places on top of the shaker where each bump is to go. Consider carefully the configuration or layout of the bumps: random, linear, and circular patterns can all look good. Bear in mind that each little bump takes up more space than just a dot, so allow room for them to fit comfortably. Pierce each marked spot with a small-gauged hole cutter.

12 To make the bumps, roll pea-sized balls of clay, then press the rounded end of a wooden stick (small paint brush handles are good) into each ball **[G]**. Form the clay down and around the sides of the stick before carefully twisting the clay off. Once the shapes have firmed up, trim them back to give yourself just the right amount of bump. This is easier to do with a really sharp, thin-bladed knife. You can make them solid by rolling a pea of clay and cutting it in half when it's firmed up. Make more bumps than you need, as there'll be inevitable casualties!

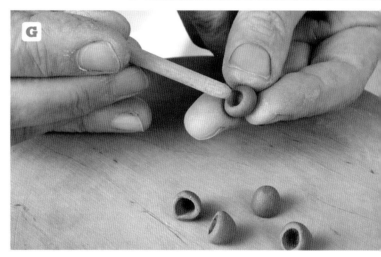

13 Slip and join each little bump so that it sits neatly over a pierced hole. When they're all firmly in place, use the hole-making tool or needle to perforate the very tops **[H]**. Don't be worried about making the holes larger than you need—when you glaze the shaker, the holes get filled with glaze, thus reducing their aperture. Reduction fired with Meloy Black glaze.

HOURGLASS SHAKERS The two cones shapes are kept equal and more rounded with a nipped-in waist. When leather hard, the incised surface was shallowly carved and the perforations are more traditional and kept flat. Glazed with Amaco PC-40 True Celadon.

COMICAL SHAKERS The two pinched sections are mismatched in scale to give a top-heavy design. The humorous quality is further enhanced by the addition of the perforated nodules that are placed in a more organic rhythm. Glazed with Amaco Velvet Underglazes and LG-10 Transparent.

ROUNDED ORGANIC SHAKERS A reversal of shapes—smaller perched on larger—makes a somewhat figurative form. Nodule perforations add a decorative, textural element. High-fired reduction stoneware, Shanners Red.

VASE

The main body of this piece is constructed from a composite egg shape. The broader end becomes the shoulders of the vase while the narrower part tapers down to the foot. A simple, barrel neck completes this classic, elegant vessel.

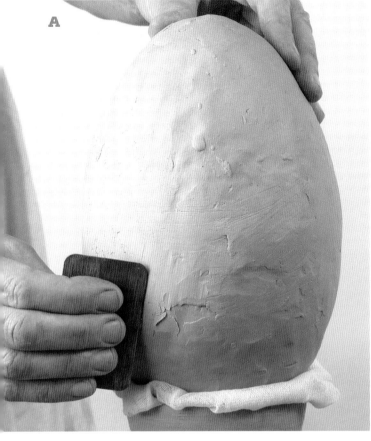

A

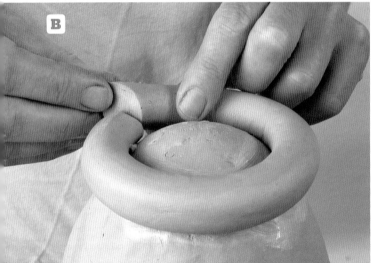

B

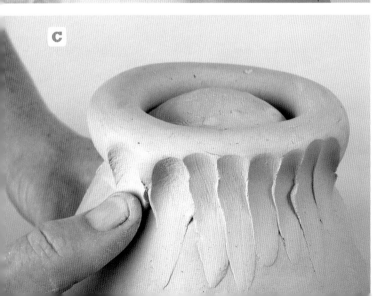

C

Pinch It

1 Prepare two fairly equal-sized lumps of clay. Pinch one into a deep, rounded bowl, the other into a tapered, more pointed bowl. While you're pinching, keep checking that the two openings have the same diameter. During this shaping stage, rest the pots intermittently so that they can stiffen up without becoming misshapen.

2 Trim the edges level, then slip and join the two pieces. Rest the piece in a nest to become firm but not leather hard.

3 If the surface is heavily textured or uneven, tidy it up a bit by scraping with a toothed tool followed by the rib [A].

4 Place the egg shape in the nest support so the more pointed end is facing up. Wrap a thick coil around the end, taking care that it's neat and level all the way around [B]. Apply plenty of slip all over the joining area and beyond. Press on the coil, feeding it around while you press from behind—this pushes out any trapped air. Don't press it on with fingertips—use the wide fleshy pad of your thumb. Fingertips can make too many dimples!

5 Thumb in the outer join so that it blends into the body of the vase [C]. Use a toothed tool to help in the shaping. Because the foot is substantial, you should be able to stand the vase up immediately, but if you're unsure, let it rest a while. Check that it's standing straight. A few sharp taps, flat and square on the table, will correct a lean.

6 To make the neck, shape a piece of clay into a longish ball and begin pinching as if for a cylinder, working at one end before turning it around and shaping the other end [D]. Keep sitting it on top of the vase to see how close you are to the desired size and proportion. Some shaping will be carried out once it's in situ, but aim to get a good, general feeling. You may need to rest it occasionally so that it can firm up.

7 When you're ready, trim back the joining end so that it's level and the correct height. Hopefully the top rim won't be too uneven and require too much trimming. Pinch out the joining end of the neck so that it flares outwards [E]. Let it stiffen until it's similar in firmness to that of the vase body.

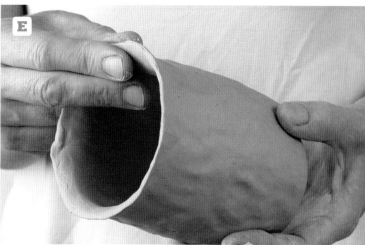

8   Place the neck in position and lightly trace around the base of it with a stick. Remove the neck and cut out the circle within the drawn area, being sure that the removed circle is at least slightly smaller than the base of the neck [F]. This creates a ledge on which the neck sits.

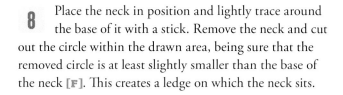

9   Slip both the cut opening and the joining end of the neck. Position the neck carefully, checking the alignment from all angles. With a tool or fingertip, gently smooth in the joining seam [G]. Add a small coil if the join looks too obvious; you want the body and neck to appear as one. If the lip of the vase is really uneven, trim it now.

10   By now the piece should be almost leather hard. Decide what kind of finish you want, then scrape, smooth, or texture as desired. I use wooden modeling tools to create a decorative repeat pattern. If there's a seam projecting inside the neck where it was joined to the body, trim it away. Make a decision about the lip: do you want it very level and thin, or full and rounded? If full and rounded is your response, add a coil now. Perhaps the natural undulation is sufficient on its own? Glazed with Amaco PC-40 True Celadon.

See pages 66-67 for vase variations.

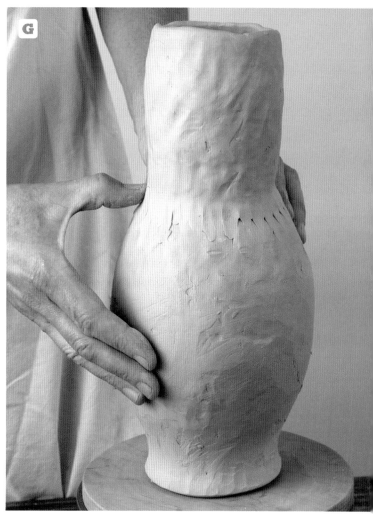

HEARTY MUG

This sturdy and substantial tankard-like mug sports a generous handle and full body. Manipulating the proportion and the style of the handle will alter the character of your mug.

Pinch It

1 I used 12½ ounces (350 g) of very soft clay to make this outsized vessel, so adjust the amount as you like. Pinch a deep funnel shape with steeply tapered walls [A]. Keep the upper rim and the base quite thick, as these will be stretched out later. Pinch the full length of the mug without the turned-out rim. Don't let the edges dry out at all!

2 Puncture through the base and pinch a little more height before turning out the opening to form the flared lip [B]. There's a distinctive waist in this upper section, so aim to keep the strong change of direction. As you're working with a soft, open-ended form, the clay, which should still be very pliable, can be a little unruly. Rest the piece to firm up, covering both ends with plastic. You may need to do this a few times throughout this shaping stage.

3 Stand the piece on the banding wheel and examine the profile carefully. Refine the shape by pushing out from the inside in areas where it needs to be fuller, and filling in any small dimples with slip and soft clay. Scrape down bumpy areas on the surface, but don't be too fastidious; more correcting can be carried out later. Check from above that both ends have a good circular shape. Keep the top rim covered in plastic, but let the rest dry to almost leather hard.

4 Pinch a disk of clay to about ⅛ inch (3 mm) thick, making sure it's wider than the base of the mug. Let it dry so that it's the same firmness as the mug.

5 Trim the wide end of the mug so that it's level. Place the mug on the clay disk and trace around the circumference of the base. Slip both the wide end rim and around the traced circle. Position the mug on the slab and give it a gentle twist in one direction—you will feel it clamp into place. Lift up the entire piece and gently give it a couple of firm taps squarely on the table; this helps strengthen the join. Wipe away any slip that's oozing out using your fingertip, not a sponge. Trim away the unwanted clay around the base of the mug [C].

6 A foot ring is optional, but I like the way it ties in with the rounded lip. Roll out a soft, even coil that's longer than the circumference of the base. Slip the outer edge of the base and carefully press on the coil so that it overhangs just a fraction. Use a wet finger to smooth where the two ends join together [D].

7 Stand the mug up, and, with a wet finger, wipe quickly around the upper part of the coil to blend it in and give it a smooth finish.

8 Check the overall surface of the mug for final blemishes.

9 If necessary, trim the lip around the top to make it level. Roll out a thin, even coil, making it longer than the circumference of the rim, to allow for trimming. Slip the top of the rim and carefully start to lay the coil into place, pushing gently from behind to join it on and to expel air as you go—careful not to over flatten [E]!

10 Smooth in the outside and inside seams with the side of your thumb, being careful not to disturb the rounded top edge. Again, a finger dipped in water and wiped quickly over the edges is a useful way of finishing this detail.

11 The handle is formed from a soft coil of tapered clay, much like a very long, skinny carrot. As always, make it longer than you need to allow for trimming. Flatten the coil by pressing a wooden board on top—but don't overdo it! Trim the coil at the thicker end; this will be attached to the lower part of the mug. Lay the handle on its side and shape into an approximate "C". Let it firm up a little before proceeding.

12 Slip both of the areas on the mug where the handle ends will join. Press on the thicker end of the handle so that it bends slightly outward. If you feel the handle is too long, trim some off, but keep some extra which will help in shaping and joining. Curve the handle upward, giving it a nice, fluid flourish, and then turn it inward at the top before pressing in into the slip [F]. Neatly trim away any excess clay. As an extra detail, I made a large dimple in the lower join by pressing a fingertip into the soft clay. Don't fiddle with the handle! Turn the mug upside down for a couple of hours to prevent the handle from sagging. Let the whole piece dry slowly under a light draping of plastic. Glazed with Arbuckle Tin with homemade and Amaco GDC majolica onglazes.

ELEGANT NOSTALGIC MUG Flip over the main project piece and you can see this shape emerging. The taller, narrower stem means you will have to keep more clay in reserve for lengthening out the form. The handle is made by laying three coils side by side and then pressing them flat. Reduction stoneware. Marshmallow glaze (interior). Meloy Black (exterior).

GUTSY TEACUP The Hearty Mug is yet again inverted but this time shortened. The big bowl has a fuller curve. The base is nipped in to echo a traditional teacup shape. It has a simple unadorned strap handle. Reduction stoneware with Marshmallow glaze.

DIMPLED MUG Similar to the Nostalgic Mug but pinched out to give a soft curve near the base, making a more complex form. The dimples were pressed in using the end of a stick and the strap handle was added last. Reduction stoneware. Heather's Celadon.

COUNTRY JUG

A curvaceous and practical vessel made from three pinch pot sections, the form is reminiscent of the medieval jugs of Europe. Ideal for holding anything from cream to juice—consider it worthy of gravy too!

Pinch It

1 First we'll make the largest shape: the full body shape of the jug. Prepare two lumps of clay that are reasonably similar in size. Pinch them into bowl shapes. Imagine a ball cut in half; these are the two shapes you'll need. Make them slightly deeper if you don't want a perfect sphere. Try and pinch them thinly in order to make a lighter jug, but keep the rims thick and level for good joining.

2 When they're firm enough, join them using slip and then blend them together at the seam. Fill in with a soft coil if necessary. While the pot is completely sealed, there's some leeway to compress and alter the shape using your palms or a wooden paddle. If the surface is heavily textured or bumpy, scrape it down so there's less finishing to do later **[A]**. Rest the piece in a nest while you start making the neck.

3 Prepare a piece of clay approximately the same size as for one of the bowls. Give it a slightly longer log shape before plunging in your thumb. Pinch into a steep-sided narrow bowl. Keep the base thick and don't let the rim become too thin **[B]**.

4 Puncture through the unopened end of the bowl. This is the base of the neck, so it should be narrower here, the complete shape being a generously flared funnel. Check the proportions of the neck against that of the jug's body, pinching it wider or taller as necessary. Note that the top of the neck is almost as wide as the body of the jug.

5 Trim the joining end of the neck so that it's both the correct length and level. Pinch it out to give it a slight flare **[C]**. This will help in joining.

6 As soon as the body shape is strong enough, decide where to place the footring. Turn it over and add a soft coil. Since the ring is quite shallow and narrow, the coil need not be fat **[D]**.

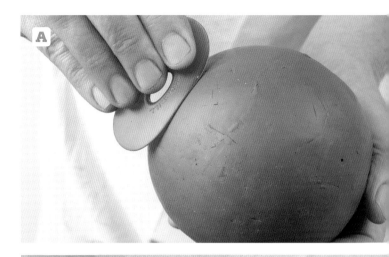

E

F

7 Sit the neck centrally on top of the sphere. Take your time finding the best position. Turn it around, viewing from several angles to make sure that it's not off center. Mark around the base of the neck [E].

8 Cut out the circle of marked clay, staying slightly inside the line that you drew [F]. Take this opportunity to clean up the inside of the jug body, smoothing and reinforcing the seam. The body should still be soft enough to push out and reshape from inside (using a round-ended tool or fingertip), if necessary. Be careful not to distort the opening.

9 Slip both pot and neck, and press gently together. Carefully smooth in the seam around the neck with your thumb, a finger, or another tool [G]. Blend it in so that it flows into the shape of the body; you want them to look connected. Now that the two parts are one, you can adjust the shape of the neck, making it wider if necessary.

10 Check that the rim is level and that there are no splits. If there are, trim it back, rounding off the cut edge with a wet finger. You can add a thin coil if you want more height.

11 In order to form the spout, it's vital that the neck is still fairly soft and pliable. Choose the placement of the spout. With thumb and forefinger on the outside, and the index finger of your other hand, press two sides of the

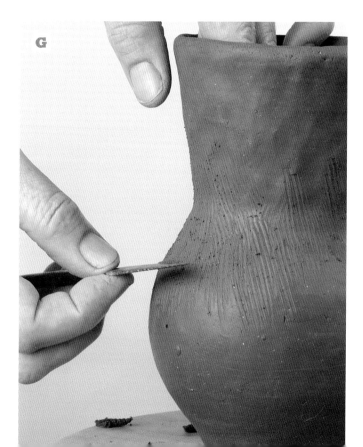

G

neck together with a sort of pinching action. Use the finger on the inside to help guide and control the shape [H]. It's quite magical the way the spout suddenly appears! Continue the pinching down the length of the neck, easing off the pressure near the bottom. This will create a "throat" to the spout rather than just a "beak." You can thin the pouring edge by drawing a wet finger along the inside of the spout.

12   Slip the base of the pot before you attach the foot, and thumb the coil in well on the outside so that it integrates with the form. Stand the jug up to check that it's level. A few sharp taps on a tabletop will correct a lean.

13   Tidy up the surface, scraping away any obvious lumps and filling dimples with slip and small beads of soft clay.

14   Before making the handle, draw a faint vertical line on the side of the pot to help in the placing of the handle. Mark also the two areas where it's to join. Make a handle and lay it on its side. Give it a curve and then let it firm up just a little; this will help facilitate the joining process.

15   Trim the coil to the approximate length. The thicker end is joined at the top and cut at about a 45° angle. Apply slip to the joining areas marked out on the pot. Press in the handle at the top, looping it down to the lower joining area (keep an eye on the vertical line you drew) [I]. Trim off the extra clay with a knife and then smooth the clay outward. Keep the piece lightly draped in plastic while the handle stiffens.

16   Trim the inside of the jug where the neck is attached. Cut back the projecting clay of the body and smooth soft clay into any deep channels. The piece featured in the main photo was dipped in white slip and then quickly wiped through with fingertips to create the stripes. Glazed with Suzi Cress's Honey glaze over white slip.

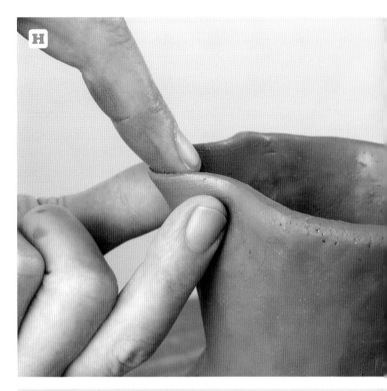

TALL BEAKED JUG A short, wide collar is added to a pinched bowl form to create a broad, practical wide-mouthed jug. The spout is pinched and shaped separately and joined well below the rim. A generous multi-grooved coil handle is added last. Glazed with Amaco HF23 with red iron oxide spot decoration.

BLUE GOURD Before cutting open, and while still fairly soft, a composite pinch pot was grooved with the side of a stick. When stiffer, it was cut open and the coil foot and straight collar added. The ropelike handle is made from a twist of several thin coils. Egyptian Turquoise glaze.

PAINTERLY JUG In essence this is the Country Jug with a less curvaceous profile. The neck is a fraction taller and straighter. A coil was added to the rim, giving a fuller, more rounded lip. Glazed with various slips under Glossy Transparent.

HORS D'OEUVRES TRAY

The number of compartments in this platter depends on your intended feast. Consider its purpose carefully and the foodstuffs that it'll likely hold, then adapt your design accordingly. Opting for an even number of "pockets" will help in the configuration. Although each one doesn't need to be identical, it'll help in the construction if they're similar in diameter.

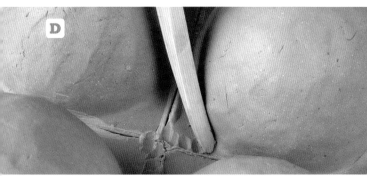

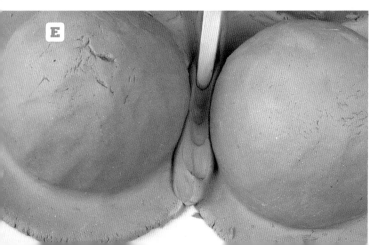

Pinch It

1   This tray has eight pockets, so I weighed out eight balls of clay, each weighing approximately 8 ounces (227 g); you can match them by eye. Keep them wrapped in plastic while you pinch the first bowl shape, leaving the rim thick, as this clay will be stretched out later.

2   When you have a good bowl shape, pinch the rim outward so that it's relatively wide and flat [A]. Don't try and perfect the entire shape all at once. Establish the basic form, then rest it rim-side down while you move on to pinch the next ball. Rest each one rim-side down so that they can stiffen up.

3   Now that they're stronger, you can refine the shapes, pinching them fuller and thinner and making the rims wider. The inside of each bowl should be pinched to have a very regular surface without big lumps or dimples— it's tremendously difficult and time consuming to work on these inside shapes once they are joined.

4   To completely flatten a rim and make a 90° angle between it and the body of the bowl, place the bowl facedown on a smooth wooden board and press the back of the rim [B]. Do the same to the other bowls. Try and keep the rims a similar thickness, as this will help at the joining stage. Let them all firm up so they aren't at all floppy, but neither do you want them leather hard.

5   Keep the bowls rim-side down and trim two sides of the four corner bowls (you're creating a 90° right angle). All the remaining bowls will have three cut sides [C]. Each bowl will retain some of the flat curved rim; these curves create a scalloped edge around the perimeter. This extra clay allows you to trim the outside edge later on.

6   When all the bowls have been cut, lay them facedown on a board covered with a nice piece of smooth cardboard or very thick paper. Arrange the pots in the order you want. You may need to trim some edges to get a tighter fit. Slip both joining edges and press down firmly, using a round-ended wooden tool or your finger if you can get it between the shapes [D]. Don't lift them up to join; do it all from behind while they lie on the wood.

7   To reinforce the joins, press thin coils of clay into the seam [E].

8 You may find that you have a few gaps between the joins and around the outside edge. Fill those in now using a little slip and plugs of soft clay [F]. Trim the outside edges so that they're reasonably straight—again, no need for a ruler.

9 To build the sides of the tray, slip one of the upper outside edges of the tray, roll out a very thick coil, and press the coil along this length [G], smoothing it in so that it's joined well. Do this all the way around [H]. Place a coil through the center to divide the interior of the tray into two halves [I]. This will provide added strength and prevent warping.

10 Pinch the coils upward, keeping them straight and reasonably level. These become the outside walls of the tray and must be high enough to exceed the tallest bowl shape, otherwise the tray will wobble [J]. Don't allow the uppermost edge to get too thin. The neater and truer the sides are now, the less tidying up you'll need to do later. Cover the interior bowl shapes with plastic and let the outside wall stiffen up so that it's as firm as the center.

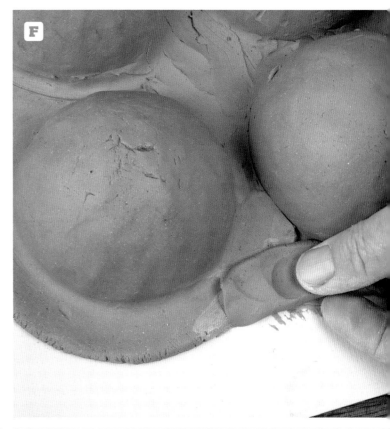

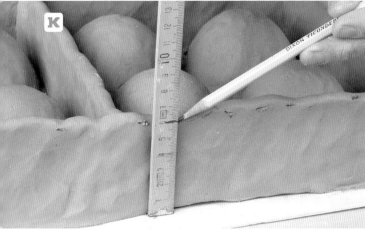

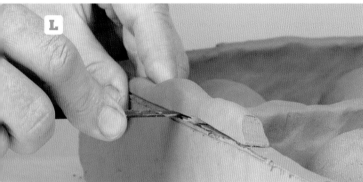

11 When the entire piece is leather hard, trim the exterior and interior walls so that they're level. You can do this by eye, but marking up the side of the wall with a ruler is more accurate [K]. Every half inch or so, mark off the desired height with a dot. Do this all the way around and then join up the dots with the ruler (remember not to cut lower than the highest bump!). Cut along the line with a sharp knife [L].

12 Before turning the piece over, spend some time smoothing and leveling the sides. Using a stiff flat piece of wood or metal (preferably one with a right angled corner), carefully shave along the outside edge [M]. The aim is to even out the surface.

13 Sandwich the tray between two pieces of wood and flip it over. Peel away the paper or card. All the joining seams will be visible. They can be interesting and worth leaving, but if you want to eliminate them, fill them in with a bit of slip and a small coil of clay [N].

14 Let the filled areas dry out a little, then scrape the entire top surface with a wide, flat rib or side of a steel ruler [O]. This will neaten up the finish and level the surface. If necessary, do the same to the flat side panels [P].

15 After the final shaving and smoothing of top and sides, use the end of a rounded stick (in this instance I used a wooden spoon) and quickly tap into the top surface to create the divots [Q]. This pleasant, tactile texture contrasts well with the smoothness of the pockets.

16 The handles are attached last. Roll two coils of clay to the correct length and thickness—it may take a few attempts to gauge the right thickness. Once you're satisfied, bend the handles into a gentle curve and leave them to firm up just a little (keep the main piece wrapped in plastic to prevent further drying). Using lots of slip, join the handles to the short sides of the tray, setting them slightly above the center line [R]. Be sure to roughen the two joining surfaces in order to help strengthen the join.

17 Refine the overall curve of the handle by running your thumb and fingers back and forth along the entire

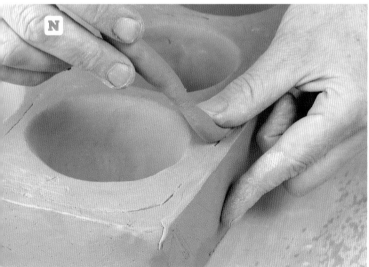

length. You should also be able to boost the join by applying more pressure as you smooth and shape where they attach. You can texture the handles now using the same tool as you did for the main surface [s]. The handles will not yet be leather hard so go easy on the tapping pressure or you'll end up with deeper holes that might look at odds with the rest! If you prefer, you can wait until they are leather hard. The piece must be dried slowly under plastic to prevent warping and cracking. Amaco PC-53 Ancient Jasper.

HORS D'OEUVRES TRAY
VARIATIONS

THE MEDIEVAL The compartments were made deeper and given a flattened base (bumped squarely on the table). Each pot has two flattened sides set at right angles, allowing the shapes to fit snugly together. It's all joined with a soft flattened coil, which continues as a broad lip around the outside edge of the piece. The small handles are made separately from soft coils, loosely shaped and flattened. Commercial stoneware glaze. Amaco PC-53 Ancient Jasper.

THE TRIPOD Each pinch pot was made wider and shallower and given an inward turning lip. Joined to each other using slip and a small reinforcing coil, they were upturned when leather hard and each bowl given one small curved leg of clay, allowing the piece to stand in secure tripod fashion. Black-and-white slip with glossy transparent glaze.

BAKING STYLED TRAY This piece begins exactly as the main project does. Once the compartments were joined and the surrounding clay trimmed to a rectangle, the piece was flipped over and a soft coil added to the outer rim. The handles were made by flattening two coils of equal size. Each coil was deeply grooved with a stick and then curved into shape. Amaco underglazes and LG-10 glaze.

COZY TEAPOT

Teapots are great fun to design and make—they really are functional pieces of sculpture that always evolve into a unique personality. This one, with its four scurrying feet, has an animal quality. Three cup-shaped pinch pots are combined to make the more sophisticated body shape. If you've made a covered jar and a mug, the only new element will be the spout.

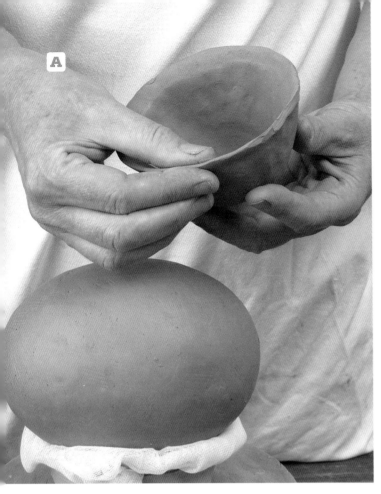

Pinch It

1 Pinch the main body mass using the composite technique (page 14)—visualize a pellet shape rather than a ball. Once the two halves are joined, check that the shape is not too full through the center. Scrape and flatten as necessary, but don't over-finish the surface; this refinement will be carried out later.

2 Pinch a pot for the top hump [A]. As it takes shape, keep checking its size against the main form, aiming to get the proportion that you sketched in your drawing. Don't compromise! When it's the same firmness as the main body, sit the hump on top of the main body and draw a line around the edge. Cut out all the clay that's inside the line.

3 Now that the form is open, you have the opportunity to clean up the join seam on the inside, and if necessary, swell out the shape from inside [B].

4 Join the two shapes, adding a coil to the outside seam if necessary so that the two sections appear as one [C].

5 Mark off on the pot the four joining areas, making sure they're evenly spaced. Make four soft balls of clay of similar size and use slip to attach them to the pot. Press them onto the underside. Smoothing and twisting them with wet fingertips helps with the shaping [D]. Take extra care to view the piece from all sides, checking that the piece is well balanced and level. Dry the feet off as you go so that they don't get crushed.

6 Draw [E] and then cut around an object of desirable size, such as a jar lid, to make a circular opening for the teapot lid [F]. Cut neatly, holding the knife at about a 45° angle. The disk you remove can be adapted into the lid.

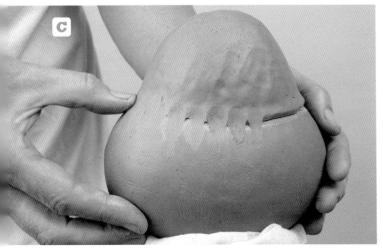

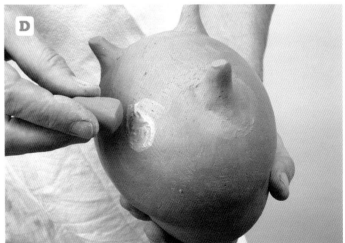

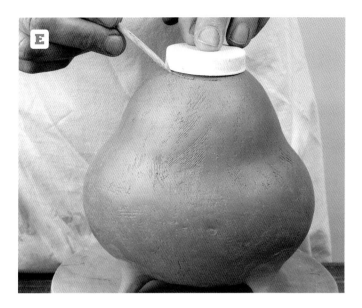

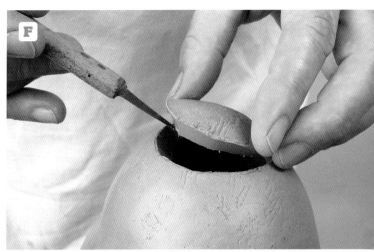

7 Fit a gallery into the teapot opening and then add a flange to the underside of the lid. Make sure the lid doesn't fit too tightly [G]. You can add the knob now or at the end of the project.

8 Use a lump of soft clay to make the spout. Modeling the spout is a gradual process of shaping, fitting, and trimming. Don't rush it. I suggest making two or three at once and keeping the best one. There is no tried and tested rule on how much clay to use. It really is trial and error, but the more you practice, the better you'll be at judging the correct quantity. Hold a smallish lump of clay up to the pot and try to imagine that clay stretched out and enlarged. Remember to allow extra for trimming.

9 Shape the piece of clay so that it's tapered, and pinch the widest end first, opening it up with the end of a finger. Pierce through the entire length using a pointed stick, and wiggle the stick in circles to enlarge the hole. Pinch and push the clay from inside, and pull and narrow the pointed end. Rest the form every so often to allow it to firm up. Don't try and model the spout all in one go; you'll have more control and better results if you do it in stages. Make the spout plump and try to keep the wider end slightly flared and thin, as this will help it to fit snugly to the pot. Before it gets too firm, create the curve in the spout by manipulating it with both hands, coaxing it gently from inside and out to give it an elegant flourish [H]. Check if the shape and proportion are correct by holding it up to the pot. If it's too thick but the shape is good, trim it from the inside, carefully shaving away the clay with a sharp knife or toothed-edged tool. A thin spout will be a better pourer!

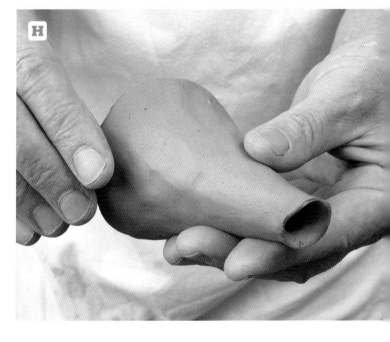

10 The end that joins to the pot needs a subtle but complex curve. Trim the angle in order to get a good fit. Cut back the narrower end if it's too long.

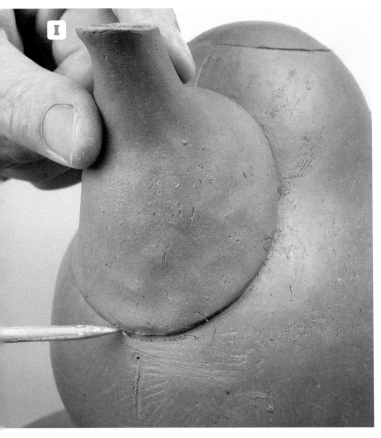

11 Sketch a vertical centerline on the front and back of the spout and also a vertical line on the pot itself. This ensures correct placement of the spout. When you're happy with your spout, line up the vertical sketch lines, double-checking the placement from several angles. Draw around the joining end [I].

12 Within the outlined area, make either one large hole or several evenly spaced holes [J].

13 Apply slip to both the spout and pot, then gently press on the spout. Smooth in the joining edge, adding a soft coil of clay to the seam if necessary [K & L].

14 The handle is a coil of clay, slightly flattened through the middle but thicker and more cordlike at the joining ends. Shape it while the clay is soft, but let it firm up a little before attaching. To get a good handle, you may need to make several [M].

15 If you didn't do it earlier, add the knob to the lid [N]. Leaving the knob until last allows you to better gauge the best size and shape to complement your piece's composition. Put a small hole through the top of the lid to help the tea flow. The teapot should be close to leather hard; finish the surface, shaving away any unwanted textures and bumps.

16 The raised design is applied before the teapot gets beyond the leather hard stage. Cut leaves, stems and flower-like motifs freehand from a thin soft slab of the same clay [O].

17 Apply each piece using slip and pat firmly into place using a wooden paddle (fingertips would leave messy dimples) [P & Q]. Reduction fired with Cushing Matt under 20th Century.

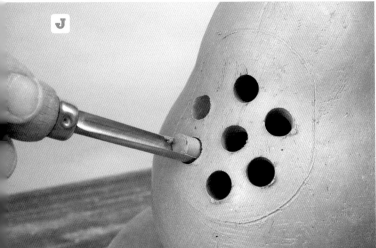

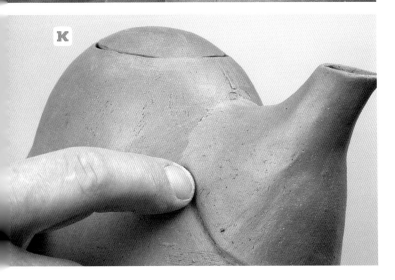

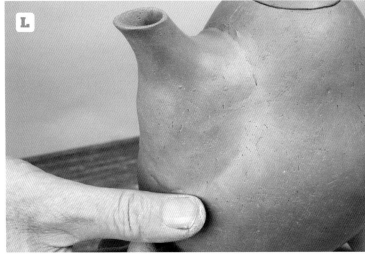

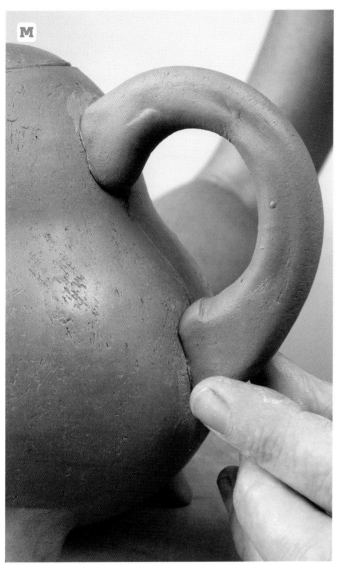

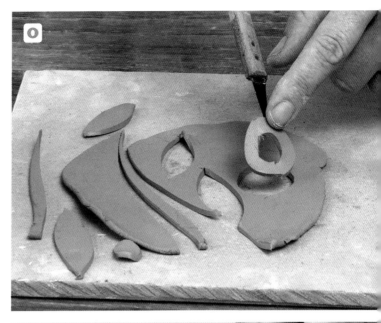

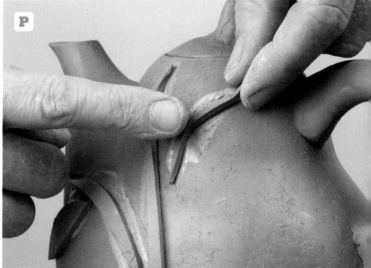

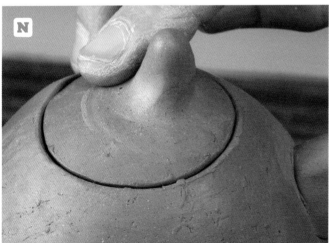

JAPANESE-STYLE TEAPOT The three-part body shape remains, but it's formed somewhat rounder. The inset lid and high arching strap handle add a new dimension. Low-fire commercial glaze Amaco A-62 Camel with wax-emulsion resist.

CHINESE-STYLE TEAPOT This shares the same composite body as the project piece, but instead of the high domed top, it sports a short collar neck and a mini convex lid. The plump "doughnut" foot gives stability and height. High-fired reduction stoneware with Shiny Black and Marshmallow glazes.

LITTLE CRUSTY TEAPOT After joining two cup shapes, various gnarly rocks were pressed into the spherical body to give a pitted texture. A thick generous handle and jaunty spout bring an animated quality to the piece. High-fired reduction stoneware with Dry Bone Ash glaze.

APPENDIX

The following pages include recipes for homemade glazes and slips. Many examples are illustrated with photos but remember, your clay, your application technique, and thickness all have a bearing on the final appearance of the glaze. Therefore, use the examples as a good guide and be prepared for exciting variations and new discoveries.

GLAZE AND SLIP RECIPES

Glaze Recipes

Samples of low-temperature glazes (earthenware) are shown on tiles made from red clay. The right side of each tile is coated with white slip to show the contrasting color response of the glaze. Each tile shows three glaze thicknesses, with the thicker application at top.

EGYPTIAN TURQUOISE, CONE 04 [A]
Gerstly borate–30g
Frit 3110–182g
Ball clay–38g
Copper carbonate–15g

GUILD HONEY, CONE 04
(semi matt)
Gerstly borate–30g
Frit 3110–182g
Ball clay–38g
Red iron oxide–27g

ARBUCKLE MAJOLICA, CONE 03 [B]
Frit 3124–65.8g
Kona feldspar–17.3g
China clay–10.8g
Nepheline syenite–6.2g
Bentonite–2g
Tin oxide–4g
Zirconium–8g

SUZI'S GLOSSY HONEY GLAZE, CONE 03
Powdered red clay–26g
Fritted lead bisilicate–68g
Cornish stone–2g
Whiting–2g

MANCHESTER SEMI-MATT TIN GLAZE, CONE 03
This has more depth and texture if used over the black slip.
Cornish stone–9.5g
Frit 3124–64g
Whiting–5g
China clay–21g
Tin oxide–7g
Titanium–3g

GLOSSY TRANSPARENT, CONE 03 [C]
Frit 3124–64.5g
Kona feldspar–17g
China clay–10.5g
Nepheline syenite–6g
Bentonite–2g

Slip Recipes

Apply to greenware. For brighter color use under the Cone 03 Glossy Transparent glaze [D].

BASIC WHITE SLIP
Ball clay–60g
China clay–40g

The following colors are made by adding oxides to the basic white slip recipe.
Blue: Cobalt 1.5–2g (increase quantities by 0.5g and upwards to intensify the color)
Mid green: Copper oxide 3g
Blue-purple: Cobalt oxide 2g, Manganese dioxide 1g

For a brighter, more extensive color palette, add 10g of commercial powdered stain to every 100g (dry weight) of the basic white slip.

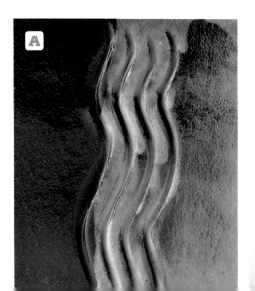
A

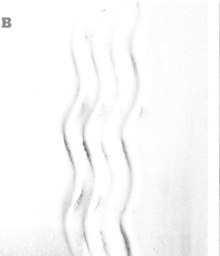
B

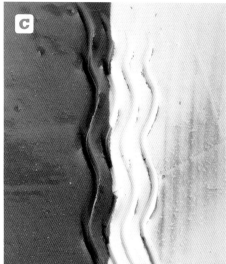
C

BLACK SLIP
Powdered red clay–85g
Manganese dioxide–6g
Cobalt oxide–4g
Red iron oxide–5g

BROWN SLIP
Powdered red clay–60g
Ball clay–40g

Onglaze Decorating Pastes

Add dry ingredients to water and push through 100 mesh sieve. The final consistency should be quite stiff and brushed on thinly like water color paint. I recommend teaspoons for measuring the volumes, as a little paste goes a long way [E].

3 parts 3124 frit
3 parts Gerstly borate
1 part powdered commercial stain

Recipes for Coloring Clay

For inlay and marbling, be sure that the base clay you are coloring is in the same family as the one you will be joining to, not just in terms of temperature but in texture; otherwise the two clays may separate during firing. The colors are more intense at high temperatures so you may want to decrease the amount of oxide, perhaps by one half. As in so many instances, testing is advisable and beneficial.

Below are the resulting colors when adding ¼ level teaspoon of oxide to 1 pound of plastic white clay:
cobalt carbonate – creates gray blues
red iron oxide – gives a golden warm brown
black iron oxide – results in gray brown
copper carbonate – creates gray greens

For further variations try combining two oxides such as:
¼ tsp cobalt carbonate + ¼ tsp manganese dioxide = purple gray blue
¼ tsp cobalt carbonate + ¼ tsp red iron oxide = earthy blue
¼ tsp copper carbonate + ¼ tsp cobalt carbonate = warm green blue

When using stains, increase the color-to-clay ratio to 1 pound clay: 1 level teaspoon stain powder.

Stoneware Glaze Recipes

Glaze samples are shown on a buff stoneware clay. White slip was applied to the right-hand side to show glaze response over a lighter body. All illustrated tiles were fired in a reduction gas kiln to cone 10. Results will be different when fired in an electric kiln.

SPOOR SLIP GLAZE, CONE 8-10 [A]

China clay–45g
Ball clay–10g
Whiting–45g
Cobalt oxide–0.5g

DRY BONE ASH GLAZE, CONE 8-10 [B]

Powdered red clay–10g
Bone ash–60g

ASHLEY'S BLUE, CONE 8-10

For exterior use only—not dinnerware safe
Barium carbonate–33.3g
Nepheline syenite–50g
China clay–16.7g
Copper carbonate–3g

CUSHING MATT, CONE 9-10

Custer feldspar–208g
Dolomite–240g
Whiting–40g
China clay–264g
Flint–48g

PLUM RED, CONE 9-10 [C]

Custer feldspar–1389g
Gerstly borate–408g
Dolomite–159g
Flint–594g
China clay–75g
Whiting–246g
Tin oxide–89g
Copper carbonate–30g

MARSHMALLOW, CONE 9-10 [D]

Custer feldspar–33.99g
Flint–22.52g
Zirconium–12.52g
Gerstly borate–11.05g
Whiting–6.71g
Talc–5.01g
Zinc–4.29g
China clay–4.20g

20TH CENTURY, CONE 9-10 [E]

Cornish stone–46g
Whiting–34g
China clay–20g
Copper carbonate–4g
Tin oxide–4g
Bentonite–2g

MELOY BLACK, CONE 9-10

Dolomite–17.8g
Whiting–3.2g
Nepheline syenite–16.2g
Custer feldspar–37.9g
China clay–24.9g
Bentonite–1g
Black iron oxide–5g
Cobalt carbonate–1g

CARIBBEAN GREEN, CONE 9-10 [F]

Custer feldspar–294g
China Clay–120g
Whiting–24g
Dolomite–114g
Zirconium–66g
Cobalt carbonate–3g
Chrome oxide–6g

SANNERS RED, CONE 9-10 [G]

Custer feldspar–527g
China clay–250g
Talc–40g
Bone Ash–40g
Whiting–210g
Red iron oxide–60g

SHINY BLACK, CONE 9-10 [H]

Ball clay–10g
Whiting–20g
Flint–30g
Kona feldspar–40g
Cobalt oxide–1g
Black iron oxide–8g
Manganese dioxide–3g

HEATHER'S CELADON, CONE 9-10 [I]

China Clay–10g
Whiting–20g
Flint–30g
Custer feldspar–40g
Robin's Egg Mason Stain–2g

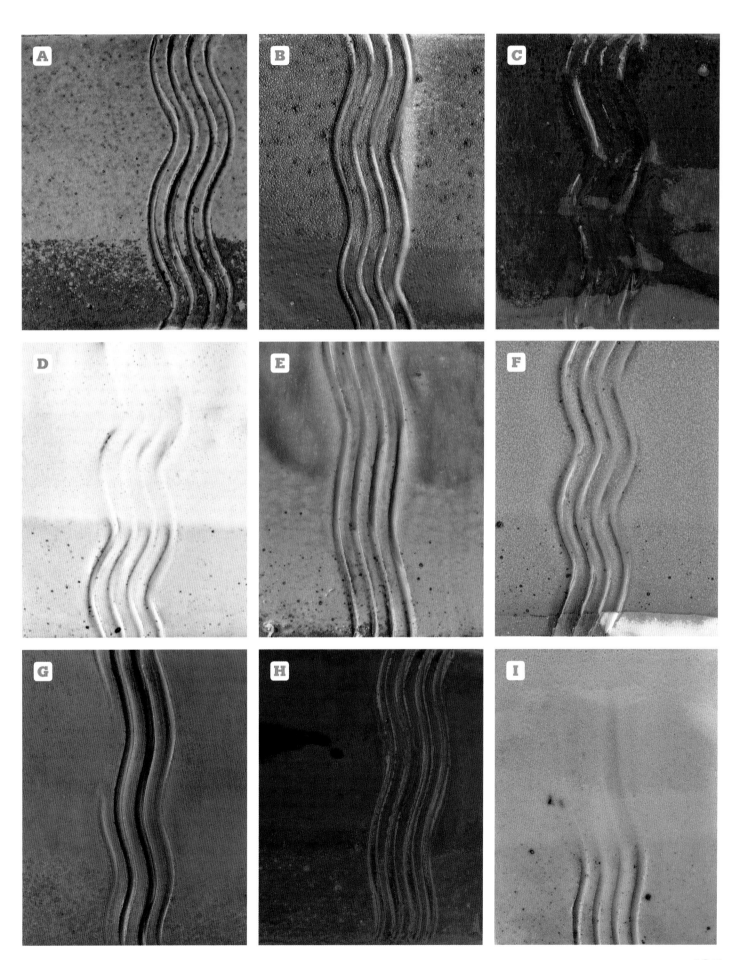

GLOSSARY

BANDING WHEEL – used to rotate a sculpture to enable a piece to be easily viewed and worked on from all sides

BISQUE – ware that has been low fired in preparation for glaze firing

BISQUE FIRING – the initial firing, heating clay in a kiln to approximately 1830°F (999°C)

BONE DRY – the state in which all the physical water has evaporated from a piece of clay

CALIPER – a tool for measuring distance

CERAMIC – clay that has been fired to a state of chemical conversion

CLAY BODIES – types of soft, prepared clays

COILING – a technique using rolled pieces of clay

EARTHENWARE – a low firing clay body or glaze

FIRING – the process of heating a clay body to result in hardening and setting of the shape

FORMING – shaping the clay

GALLERY FITTING – horizontal ledge built in to the upper inside portion of a pot to support a lid

GLAZE – a liquid that's applied to clays and that, after firing, seals, smooths, and colors the clay body's surface

GREENWARE – any shaped, unfired clay

HACKSAW BLADE – narrow metal strip with a fine-toothed edge that can be snapped into smaller pieces for convenience (wear eye protection when snapping)

INLAY – the decorative process of carving into clay and filling the incisions with slip or colored clay

KILN – a piece of equipment in which clay is baked

LEATHER HARD – the stage at which clay is firm but yields to the pressure of tools

MAJOLICA – white glazed earthenware usually decorated with oxides or onglazes

OXIDES – naturally occurring minerals used to color slips, clays, and glazes

PINCHING – a technique that involves squeezing clay with your fingers to make a shape

PLASTIC – the state of clay that is soft and malleable enough to bend, fold, and squeeze without cracking

PORCELAIN – a smooth, white, slippery clay that, when high fired, is hard and dense, with a glasslike quality

RESIST – commonly liquid wax or paper used to create decorative surface patterns by masking off areas of the pot

SGRAFFITO – decorative technique of carving through slip after it's become leather hard to expose the clay color below it

SLAB – a smooth, flat piece of clay resulting from being rolled with a rolling pin

SLIP – liquid clay that can be colored with stains or oxides. Also, the "glue" used in joining clay together.

STAINS – similar to oxides except not as powerful, stains are commercially manufactured and used to color slips, clays, and glazes

STONEWARE – a dense mid- or high-range clay body, glaze, or firing

TOUCH DRY – not sticky when touched but not fully dry

UNDERGLAZE – liquid ceramic pigment applied to greenware or bisqueware for decorative effects

VITRIFICATION – fusion of the clay body resulting in dense, watertight clay

Reference Materials

A POTTER'S BOOK
Bernard Leach
Approaches to design and decoration

FINDING ONE'S WAY WITH CLAY
Paulus Berensohn
Making larger forms and clay coloration

MARY ROGERS ON POTTERY AND PORCELAIN
Mary E. Rogers
Coloring clay and working with porcelain

THE POTTER'S DICTIONARY OF MATERIALS AND TECHNIQUES
Frank and Janet Hamer
Comprehensive technical information regarding clays, kilns, and firing

ACKNOWLEDGMENTS

I would like to extend my gratitude to the following people for their help with this book:

Special thanks to John Cowen and Tim Heffernan of Sheffield Pottery of Massachusetts (Sheffield-pottery.com) for donating all the clays used in this book. A broad selection of clay types was needed to create the projects and their variations and to extend the glazing possibilities. Sheffield was able to provide a wonderful selection of first-class plastic clays. Mass White Moist and #107145 are the two earthenware bodies used, as well as three exceptional stoneware clays: T1, #42, and #95400. The porcelain is #92700. I'm indebted to the team not only for their generosity but also for their technical help with selecting the right clays for the job in hand.

Sincere thanks to Diana Faris of Amaco (amaco.com) for generously providing so many of the wonderful glazes used on several of the project pieces. Amaco is truly a pottery/craft supplier and pioneering glaze specialist. Their tremendous range of glaze colors, textures, and firing temperatures is unsurpassed, so I was thrilled to have such a wide variety of outstanding material to select from. Glazes from the following ranges are featured throughout the book: Potter's Choice Liquid Glazes (PC Series), Artist's Choice Liquid Glazes (A Series), Sahara (HF Series), Velvet Underglazes (V Series), Matte Liquid Glazes (LM series), GDC Majolica Gloss Decorating Colors (GDC Series) and Liquid Gloss Glazes (LG Series).

A thousand thanks go to Linda Kopp, my wonderful editor at Lark, for her tireless support, patience, and enthusiasm. Also at Lark, designer Kristi Pfeffer and copyeditor Alexander Alesi deserve thanks for their meticulous work on this project.

I'm indebted to John Polak, for his outstanding photography. He's the only person I know who can transform a pot of brushes into an object of desire.

Thanks also to my husband, Chris, for his support on all fronts. His technical expertise was invaluable, as was his sympathetic listening ear.

I'm grateful to Anne Connell at the Silvermine Arts Center in New Canaan, Connecticut, for saying yes to all of my requests. Also at Silvermine, clay artist and kiln-firing genius Heather Houston met my avalanche of favors with enthusiasm and good cheer. I can't thank you enough.

Potter Posey Bacopoulos provided advice and motivation.

And finally, a heartfelt thank you goes to the glorious Forbes Library in Northampton, Massachusetts. This great institution provided me the space, resources, and peace and quiet necessary for writing this book. I couldn't have done it without you.

AUTHOR BIO

Susan Halls has exhibited widely throughout the United Kingdom, the United States, and Europe. Her work has been included in the Sackler Foundation; the Victoria and Albert Museum, London; Aberystwyth University, Wales; the Shigaraki Ceramic Center, Japan; and the Contemporary Art Society, London. Susan received her Masters of Arts in ceramics from the Royal College of Art, London. She continues to teach workshops throughout the United States and the United Kingdom. She is the author of *Ceramics for Beginners: Animals & Figures* (Lark, 2011) and lives in Easthampton, Massachusetts.

Photo by Valerie Murphy

INDEX

I would like to dedicate this book to the two Valeries.